Bread

Upon

The Waters

Order this book online at www.trafford.com
or email orders@trafford.com

Most Trafford titles are also available at major online book retailers.

Printed in the United States of America.

ISBN: 978-1-4669-6640-6 (sc)
ISBN: 978-1-4669-6642-0 (hc)
ISBN: 978-1-4669-6641-3 (e)

Library of Congress Control Number: 2012920539

Trafford rev. 10/31/2012

 www.trafford.com

North America & international
toll-free: 1 888 232 4444 (USA & Canada)
phone: 250 383 6864 ♦ fax: 812 355 4082

Dedication

I dedicate this book, first of all, in loving memory of my mother and to my beloved family, students, and the kindred spirits, genuine pearls, who illuminated my path along the way.

Acknowledgements

My deepest thanks to Trudy Draper for, without her help this book would never have become a reality. Through endless hours of dedication and work, she has helped me to immortalize my mother.

Table of Contents

PROLOGUE

When I first attempted to write this narrative I was obsessed with the compulsion to immortalize a woman whose life was entirely dedicated to the well being of others. Her compassion for the suffering and her generosity for those in need was unsurpassed. Lacking every material means necessary for the comfort of daily living, she managed to share every morsel of her menial store with those who, supposedly, were in greater need. Even now, years afterwards, as I relate some of the most outstanding episodes in her life, the nobility of character which inspired this sacrificial and selfless existence seems incomprehensible.

Men and women have become famous because of some outstanding contributions they have performed in the service of mankind. In many cases they become celebrities in acknowledgement of one single meritorious deed. Yet there are others who have dedicated their whole lives to the succor of the needy and the oppressed, their labor and compassion never to be lauded or even recognized. They are the unknown; they die in unmarked graves, their noble deeds, their tales, buried with them forever.

Thus this story was, at its inception, a humble endeavor to commemorate one such meritorious soul - one single soul among the multitudes. Those into whose lives I can only cast a fleeting glimpse. Then as the tale began to unfold I realized with chagrin, that my whole narrative was a betrayal - a betrayal to those who also led valiant lives (and yes, were heroes). They were those who shared the same entourage, the same milieu, therefore faced the same grueling trials and impossible obstacles. Together they were responsible for and influenced the well being, indeed the very survival of everyone compelled to combat the rigors of the environs and untamed nature.

It became obvious that there existed not one valiant, but a battalion, up above the firmament, the pounding rhythm of their marching beat a thundering cry of protest clamoring to be heard.

It is also quite obvious that no man is an island unto himself. All his ideals, comportment, morality, living standards, the means by which he provides for his needs are affected by those in his immediate surroundings. He is somewhat a conglomeration of those who have been part of and have been influential in his life. The mind learns, gains, assimilates bits and pieces of knowledge from every acquaintance, every associate, indeed everyone, whether they be close relationship or otherwise. It abounds in the treasures thus assembled, and luxuriates in the lavish acquisitions it has accumulated. It becomes an aggregation of all the enlightenment, understanding that dwells in the spirits of those whose milieu it has shared. Thus its horizon is broadened, rises above the narrow shackles of the "self" and transcends the constrains of its immediate perspective.

Thus (from these observations) it is my presumption that my mother's essence was imbued and consumed by an amalgamation of wisdom synonymously inspired by those who surrounded her, and derived from her insatiable readings. It is with this assumption that I dare cast a glimpse into her profound, complex personality and venture to analyze the intensity, the fervor of her passions.

It is also my intent, in these unpretentious lines, that I wish, in gratitude, to celebrate the memory of those who shared our joys, our struggles and our sorrows during those difficult, yet extraordinarily euphoric times.

I deeply regret that of those who have touched my life so profoundly I can only catch mere glimpses and relate only fleeting moments of their lives.

It would indeed be gratifying if by some bizarre hazard it were possible to know and understand totally what lies hidden in the hearts of those around us. Thus to be able to share the thoughts, the turmoil, the passions, the aspirations and the rapture that transpire and lie rooted within the abyss of their souls. Unfortunately, this privilege is a fantasy, the figment of a rambling, overactive imagination. Beyond the bounds of all possibility. Yet, were it feasible, how fascinating it would be to witness intellectually each journey as one pursues his way along life's sensational, untrodden path. To be able to capture the intensity of his passions as he wanders along the way! All this is fantasy! For the depth and complexity of the human essence is unfathomable. Yet, this knowledge would dispel misunderstandings, prejudices, hatred, and false accusations! A utopia?

I apologize to you, oh ye who have preceded me in the great beyond! I cannot recapture the moments that once were within my grasp, and so my humble lines cannot do justice and acclamation to your true valor! I have often wondered why one discovers and fully appreciates so many things too late.

INTRODUCTION

It is my most profound aspiration in these humble lines, to pay tribute to the memory of my parents, especially to that of my mother. It is also my genuine desire to celebrate the memory of those who had such a formidable influence in my parents' lives. Ultimately, transcending and firmly embedded in this narrative, is the intense desire to immortalize one whose extraordinary wisdom and courage will forever guide and enlighten my path: my mother.

The drama, however, cannot be unfolded without its historical background. That is because the events that emanated and transpired in the early 20th century in Eastern Canada, the United States and Western Canada were monumental and instrumental in the shaping of my parents' childhood and future destiny.

Indeed the whole story is rooted and intermingled with the history of Quebec, the States and the early settlement of the West.

Crossing the boundary between Canada and the States was apparently not restricted in the late 19th and early 20th century. More desirable living standards, superior working conditions, and higher wages attracted many Canadians to seek employment south of the border. My grandparents on both sides of the family gravitated back and forth across the line. They remained in the location wherever the conditions and demand for labor was more advantageous. They worked in cities where there were woolen and cotton factories. Sometimes they worked as longshoremen, loading and unloading ships in the harbor. In fact, as both Canada and the States were developing countries, there was an abundance of employment available.

On my father's side of the family, it appears that as soon as they became adults the men worked in the lumber industry. They worked in various states south of the border. Connecticut, Maine, Massachusetts, New Hampshire were often the location of the stories that emerged from these days. My Dad also worked in the Canadian lumber industry. Many of the celebrities he raved about were Canadian heroes.

I am uncertain as to the kind of work my grandfather Savard did while he lived in the States. I have the impression that he must have worked in large cities. My mother recounted many stories relating to episodes that occurred while the family lived in Brooklyn. These stories always centered around unique neighbors and pleasurable adventures.

When my grandfather returned to Canada he joined the crew of men who constructed the transcontinental railway. He was there when they laid the last spike in British Columbia in 1885.

These frequent relocations must have been very difficult for the children. They must have felt displaced and insecure being constantly in unfamiliar surroundings. There was no evidence of this, however, as the tales relative to these days were filled with happiness and enjoyment. Perhaps the love of adventure and excitement compensated for any discomfort entailed.

Acknowledging that the continual displacement in search of employment did not prove detrimental to the children's welfare. There were, however, other monumental circumstances that had serious repercussions. These circumstances had far-reaching consequences influencing and defining the opportunities and prospects the future held for them.

As previously stated, in the later part of the 19th and even at the beginning of the 20th century, both Canada and the United States were developing countries. Both were in the process of settlement and political organization. Granted, the States were more advanced, therefore provided more favorable opportunities. However, both countries had problems to resolve. Many of these issues were of monumental significance. They had crucial consequences on the welfare of future generations. These issues had to be handled wisely, with scrupulous deliberations in their resolutions and implementation. Unrestricted crossing of the border between the two countries was one matter to be decided. This matter was, to the general population, beneficial, as it provided more employment opportunities. It also provided the unrestricted trading of merchandise.

The second issue was more staggering and had far-reaching consequences. This was the formidable task of the implementation and enforcement of compulsory education. Although the authorities made a concerted effort to put it into effect, the opposition of the general public rendered its realization almost an impossibility.

I am enclosing an excerpt by Charles Phillips in the Development of Education in Canada and also one by Lee C. Deighton in the V.2 Encyclopedia of Education which clearly demonstrate the horrendous task both governments faced in trying to resolve the complex situation.

During the late 19th century the provinces were making an effort to enforce attendance in public schools. The lack of cooperation of the parents who thought children should contribute to the support of the family and chores were more important than education. In Ontario 1871 the last remaining school districts were required by law to provide free education for all children. Parents were obliged legally to have their children attend school. Employers were prohibited from employing children of school age - attendance officers were employed. But the law remained only partially operative - 23% of school age children failed to attend the minimum annual period of 100 days. In 1891 penalties were imposed for parents who failed or refused to comply and employers who hired children who should have been in school.

In Quebec the issue was raised on several occasions but it was claimed to be unnecessary, even as late as 1912, as the attendance was the highest daily attendance in relation to pupils enrolled - that still left many children without an education.

1870's to 1880 the States rediscover illiteracy. There was controversy between the pros and cons regarding compulsory education. There was contention over compulsory school attendance laws. It was on the books but not obeyed. Laws were instituted in state after state but disregarded well beyond the 1900's. They were ignored by parents for economic reasons. Employers, labor unions and welfare agencies had to coordinate their efforts before written laws could be applied. Child labor laws, work permits, welfare payments and frequent school census reports were needed.

The parents' objection to school attendance had economic ramifications. They maintained that every member in a household must contribute to its support. Wages derived from the labor of all members were crucially needed for the family's survival. Therefore, the educational issue emanated from an even more formidable complication. It stemmed from and was deeply rooted in the controversial child labor problem. One was synonymous to the other. If the young attended school they could not work in factories or other institutions and contribute to the support of the family. Both authorities on educational research firmly support this theory which is self-evident.

It was during this era and these circumstances that my parents existed. In each family the manner in which the parents coped and dealt with the situation was entirely different. The decision was based, of course, on the individual philosophy and priorities of those involved.

At the time, and in my father's family, economic survival was given precedence over education. Basic needs of food, shelter and clothing had to be provided. Each member had to cooperate and contribute to supply these needs. It was imperative to the welfare of the whole household. The children were allowed to quit school at a very young age and work. It was a decision that was greatly appreciated by the young of the household, especially my Dad. His words still ring very distinctly in my memory as he declared with great emphasis and passion, "I hated school! I despised it! As soon as I could I quit. Good riddance!" And that was that! For him it meant freedom! Looking back, did they realize that they had been released from one prison (so they thought) to be imprisoned forever in a dungeon from which there is no release; the exigency that necessitates the dictates of perpetual labor.

On the other hand, to my Grandfather Savard, food for the mind transcended all other needs. His priority was the education of his children. Even when it was not compulsory, every child in the household diligently attended school. When he became skeptical concerning the quality of the public educational system, the children were transferred to private schools or convents. These schools were renown for the excellent quality of their educational programs. They were also renowned for the excellence of their teachers. Although tuition and residential fees were more than reasonable, it was an enormous drain on the household budget; yet my grandfather insisted that the children's' education must supercede all other objectives.

Thus it was that two extremely intelligent individuals in the midst of almost identical circumstances journeyed along remarkably divergent paths. A path that culminated into an entirely conflicting genre of life.

Years later, when they became acquainted, it would not have been prejudicial to render an unbiased conclusion that except for their remarkable intelligence, they were incompatible and did not belong in the same world.

Many years had gone by then. Eventful, adventurous years in which both families experienced innumerable joys and sorrows. During those years the grandparents Savard lived in the States and consequently the older members of the family married and settled in that country. We know little of their whereabouts, except that they are scattered throughout the States. Aunt Emma was the only one who corresponded with her parents. She owned a property on the States side of Niagara Falls. I deeply regret not having had the pleasure of knowing the older members of the Savard family - the aunts and uncles who decided to make their homes south of the border.

Eventually, many years later, both families returned to Canada. My Dad's family settled near "Lac St. Jean" (Lake St. John). Years later my Aunt Emma came west to visit her parents. Although she spoke mostly about her children, she did bring us news about those who had remained in the States: Joe Louis, Neil. She also spoke of the sad fate of Hélène. How I yearn to recollect the tales of their lives. It is too late - my recollections are but sketchy.

EARLY YEARS

As previously stated, this story is rooted and intermingled with the history of Quebec, the United States, and the early settlement of the West. It is a story of courage, of heroism, and nobility of character engrained in the soul of not only one spirit, my mother, but of all those who made up her world.

She was one of the youngest members of a large French Canadian family then living in the States. She had two brothers immediately older and two brothers younger than herself. It is not surprising that she was a genuine and self proclaimed tomboy; being constantly in the company of male companions. Always competing, imitating, and following four brothers can be quite hazardous, to say the least. It can also gain the ire of both the male siblings and the parents. Climbing, jumping over fences, listening in on the boys' secret plots, running barefooted through the muddy fields, is to mention a fraction of the mischievous exploits in which she delighted and which got her constantly in trouble. Her notorious adventures soon earned the culprit the reputation of being a pest. When her physical capacity proved inadequate, she used her cunning and superior intelligence to prevail over any opponent, either male or female.

It is little wonder that the parents, being extremely traditional and adhering to severe moral propriety, were utterly overcome by the unconventional behavior of their daughter. Especially as the two older daughters were perfect ladies in all aspects of manners, dress, and behavior. Both gifted in music, they were often requested to play in concerts produced by an orchestra.

This parental concern did not, however, trouble our little lady in the least. She knew that her gifts far surpassed any petty misdemeanor of which she might have been culpable.

Her gregarious nature led to the most significant, momentous episode in my grandfather's home, and hence to the starting point in my story. This episode had crucial and far-reaching consequences for the family, both economically and psychologically. The following is a brief account of the events as they transpired.

She was four, my mother, her first day in kindergarten. Seated at the supper table was a very proper, very Victorian family, my grandfather's. Suddenly, out of the blue, and out of this child's mouth came a profane, vulgar utterance, the likes of which were unheard, let alone spoken in such a milieu. Thunderstruck, the members of the family held their breath in terror, dreading my grandfather's reaction. The whole family was aware that although he was a great man, my grandfather had an explosive, violent temper. "Never, never," he thundered, pounding on the table, overwhelmed with fury, "never again will any child of mine attend any school but private schools. I will not permit any member of my family to be exposed to such vulgarity and outrageous behavior."

And so it was that the whole family attended very elite, Christian boarding schools. The decision was to have a most profound influential impact on the lives and future of school age students involved and the family as a whole. The cost of financing private residential schools was exorbitant, both in the States and in Canada. It was especially so as during the later part of the 19th century, private schools did not receive any grants and were not sponsored by the government in any form.

Private schools were self-sufficient and entirely responsible for their operational funding. Therefore the parents of children residing at the school had to pay full tuition and residential fees, in addition to the compulsory education taxes imposed by the public school system.

The economical ramifications emanating from grandfather's decision were staggering. Especially as he was a laborer and the family depended entirely on his wages for support. But he never wavered, the education of his children was paramount. The privations and sacrifices involved were endured in silence. My grandfather had spoken and his word was never questioned. The future attested that the wisdom of that decision was immeasurable.

It was while my grandfather was working south of the border that my mother, at four, first entered the convent (as private schools were called).

When the family returned to Canada, she attended a convent at Roberval and completed her studies there. It is not known when this transfer occurred. It was inconsequential, as the quality of instructions was impeccable on either side of the border.

These private residential schools were under the auspices of the Catholic Church and were managed by sisters or nuns. These devoted teachers expected excellence in both the personal and academic development of their students. The academic fields were strongly stressed. Vigilant attention was also devoted to propriety in manners, character development, positive attitudes and relationships. Instructions in musical theory, performance and vocal, plus art, needlework and drama formed part of the curriculum.

Such a comprehensive program of studies required long hours of exhausting preparations and practice, besides endless periods without leisure or rest. Such devotion is surely beyond the call of duty! Or perhaps they too have (the teachers) joined the throng of unsung heroes!

It is not clear whether the musical instructions and other extra curricular activities were included in the general fees or if they involved additional costs. The advantages to the students, however, more than compensated for the sacrifices involved. At graduation, every student played a musical instrument proficiently, had considerable vocal training, and was fully competent in the basics of musical theory.

These instructions were greatly appreciated in my grandfather's family. It brought immeasurable joy and gratitude when the two older sisters Emma, a pianist, and Hélène, a violinist, played in concerts.

My mother was perhaps the one who benefited the most from these musical and dramatic instructions. Although her expertise was as a pianist, she could, and managed to play almost any instrument within her reach. But her most extraordinary gift (talent) was in the quality and beauty of her singing voice. For often her spirits would take flight and retreat in the magical sanctuary of the ecstatic, lyrical, and melodic world of songs. And there it remained suspended in rapture, oblivious to the harshness of merciless reality. Her passion for music and song was an obsession. She had this uncanny ability to become entirely engrossed, completely immersed in the exotic realm of melody and momentarily escape into the fantasy of an illusive harmonious haven. Years later this melodious sanctuary brought immeasurable solace in times of stress.

Indeed this passion for music and song turned out to be her salvation. For often, when the futility of the situation became insufferable, she retreated into her world of music and songs or assumed the identity of a character in the illusive fantasy of her books. And so she sang. Melodious refrains poured forth from the very depths of her soul. The wonders of nature, the joy of the nightingale's trill, whose song echoes the rapture of celestial delight, the beauty of the rose in the magnificence of its bloom, the innocence of the child, the radiance of the celestial kingdom, all sprang forth, lightly, full of ecstasy and rapturous joy, in glorious melodies from her heart.

The theme of her songs was drawn from immeasurable sources. From France, the ancestral lyrics were bathed in patriotism, an obsessive loyalty and love of country, ("L'amour de la Patrie") heroism, and valor in times of war. From America, the melodies also expressed sincere patriotism but were in a lighter vein. This was also true of English melodies. Most American and Canadian themes exalted the bounteous gift of life itself. In that extraordinary repertoire, there was even a Chinese chant she had learned from a Chinese boy while living in Brooklyn, New York. This boy lived next door. He sat on the fence post separating the two properties and constantly, continually sang that same chant. Although the meaning was entirely incomprehensible to her, she was enchanted by the beauty of the melodious air. The words of the song seemed to express melancholy and deep longing for his native land across the wide expanse of the sea.

Besides patriotic songs, many others were bathed in religious and political themes. Some were in a desperate protest against oppression, prejudice, exploitation, violence, and unrequithed love. Myriads mourned the horror, the tragedies and the lunacy of war. The desperate cry of a grief stricken mother illustrates the protest emanating from most of these. "Maudit soit la guerre. Ils ont tué mon enfant. Ton fils Caan vient de tuer son frère. Cést un hero, il dort dans un cercueil." Unquestionably these words expressed the insanity, the inhumanity and barbarism of war. Thus there was a continual message incessantly weaving its way through these songs, "Man is abundantly endowed with wisdom and the faculty of speech! These weapons are far more formidable, more lethal, more powerful, than the weapons of destruction and violence. Must he continually revert to the macabre savage animal behavior in order to solve his problems."

There were also countless popular country and folk songs. Ballads, lullabies, jingles. Some of the repetitious jingles were meant to be comical and were somewhat crude, with a touch of provincialism. Usually these were nonsensical, hilarious, more like the "chantey" meant for sailors and revelers in a bar.

In contrast to the depth and beauty of the themes from my mother's sophisticated repertoire, these "chanteys" seemed almost uncouth, unpolished and did not do justice to her refined musical talent. The inclusion of simple common melodies, chants emanating from the laboring class, stemmed from my mother's abhorrence for class distinction and segregation. She could not tolerate the classification of human beings into neat little packages. Society's tendency to exclude and ostracize certain individuals or groups was repugnant to her.

Emanating from her inexhaustible lyrical volume, my mother had a song that complemented and was in harmony with every activity or situation. Picking strawberries, spinning, strolling and admiring the beauty of nature, there was always a melody appropriate to the project at hand, work or play. This never failed to create an atmosphere of animation, pleasure and cheerfulness.

Thus the joy, the rapture of music and song provided my mother with an indubitable respite from the insufferable deprivations of pioneer life. And so she incessantly escaped into the comfort and rapture of her beloved enchanting world of music and song, to soothe the misery and longing in her aching heart.

She played the piano with the same intense emotional fervor, becoming entirely absorbed in the melody and lyrical content of the composition. She found it intolerable when, in the interpretation of a chef d'oeuvre, a performer failed to empathize with the composer, thus was unable to capture the sentiment, the ecstasy the author had experienced in the creation of his work.

"Played the piano, the instrument as if it were a box", she lamented ruefully.

Surprisingly, some of these musicians had years of training and were well qualified.

Unfortunately they lacked the imagination and the sensitivity to be captivated by the melodious enchantment music encompasses.

Her musical talent was soon recognized and appreciated in the community. As a result she became the Choir Master at our local church. She enjoyed training the vocalists in the choral group. She also enjoyed guiding and directing those who played the violin in the choir.

The journey to the church was difficult as we lived seven miles away. During the winter months, the extreme cold weather compounded the hardships, as travel that far in a horse drawn sleigh was hazardous in temperatures ranging from 30 to 40 degrees below zero.

Money being non-existent, this task fulfilled a dual purpose. It was an outlet for my mother's magnificent gift as a musician and also the family's contribution to the support of the church.

Besides directing the music at the church, my mother often gave instruction on the basic musical theory and voice production.

As a musician, her most significant contribution to the community was in the process of producing and directing musical productions or concerts for the church. Most of the spectacles and dramatic performances required musical competence, both as a performer and as a director. She not only trained the actors the musical role they had to play, but often times had to do the singing for them while hiding behind the curtains.

Besides her amazing dramatic and musical talent, that amazing, extraordinary woman was a born leader. An artistic, intellectual, and spiritual leader. She participated in all community functions. When she was unable to be actively present her counsel was solicited.

She served in many public functions, acting as a justice of peace - the voluminous law books proudly displayed upright on the tall clothes cupboard. She was also a member of the school board. In a public assembly or public meeting, she was always treated with respect and admiration. Her superior education, understanding of human nature, and unwavering sense of justice, more than compensated for her modest attire.

Whenever a difficult legal document was to be completed, or an important letter involving a delicate matter had to be written, local people sought her expertise. She coached oral presentations and recitals.

Local families often asked my mother to give their children music lessons and voice training. She always tried to conform to their wishes. That however was a chore that she detested vehemently. The constant repetition with little progress drove her insane. Some individuals are tone deaf and no amount of training seems to alter that fact. Discord to a music lover is unbearable. To a musician it is torture, and this lady was not a teacher. She loathed teaching with a passion. "I would scrub walls rather than teach a classroom full of children," she claimed. Is it possible that a person with superior intelligence cannot comprehend the level of understanding and enlightenment at which someone less capable envisions the world? A fact that is clearly obvious to a genius can be most obscure and utterly inscrutable to one of lesser ability. This, of course, is the consequence of great frustration for both student and teacher.

Evidently that explains why those with the greatest minds and the most inquisitive thirst for knowledge are not the greatest teachers. They are fixated on one quest alone, the magnanimous search for truth and enlightenment. They cannot tolerate impediments in the pursuit of their vision, their dream!

That was my mother's passion, unmistakably. In order to satisfy this passion, this quest, she incessantly consumed volumes of books, magazines and newspapers. In fact, anything that displayed the printed word. Her voracious appetite for reading was insatiable. It was manifested in every aspect and minute of her existence. She even read the labels on food containers during meals - peanut butter jars, catsup bottles - the whole shebang.... Indeed the most amazing was her ability to read, even in the most precarious situations.

There is a vision that remains eternally engraved in my memory. In my mind's eye she is seated there, entirely immersed into the volume she is reading, totally absorbed, a broad smile illuminating her face. A look of pure delight enveloping her whole countenance! She is incognizant of "whatever is happening" around her. And occasionally "whatever was happening" was absolute pandemonium, absolute chaos! Dishes rattling, people arguing (sometimes even fighting), or laughing. Some shouting in an effort to be heard to drown out the noise. The very walls vibrating! Astonishing! Entirely inconceivable that anyone could concentrate in such a bedlam!

One day I mustered up the audacity to ask her how she accomplished that miraculous feat. "Well," was her extraordinary reply, "if I didn't read, they would have taken me away (to the mental hospital) years ago."

Jeannette Romaniuk

In that simple statement lies volumes of psychological wisdom. In those lines, the world of books, she escaped the harsh, unrelenting reality, and fled to the realm of illusive fantasy where she momentarily dwelt in ecstasy.

HISTORY/CAREER

At seventeen, having completed the entire academic course of studies required by the provincial educational system, my mother graduated with honors. The program of studies she had followed was extremely exigent. It included the history of Canada, France, the United States and "L'histoire Sainte" (the holy history) which was memorized word for word. The mastery of religious dogma was severely stressed. In addition to all these studies, she was fully competent in music, drama and voice production. She had received instructions in both English and French languages and was perfectly bilingual. She had the necessary teacher's qualifications and certifications. These allowed her to teach in the provincial schools of Quebec at the beginning of the 20th century.

Her career as a teacher began in Montreal. She taught for two years in that great city. The recollection of those years did not bring joyful (fond) memories. The classrooms were inordinately overcrowded. There were sixty students in her class. Instructions in both English and French languages were compulsory, half the allotted time schedule was therefore devoted to studies in each language. "It was an impossible situation," she lamented ruefully! "All I could and managed to do was to hear each day every student read his or her lesson once in both languages." It is amazing that she was able to accomplish such an extraordinary achievement!

A modern classroom with thirty students is considered overcrowded, with little hope of successful educational achievement. At the time teacher's salaries in that province were $12.00 monthly. The lodgings however were extremely reasonable, e.g. $4.00 monthly. A teacher had the exorbitant total of $8.00 to spend! On luxuries? Yet, at the time that amount may have been a most significant sum.

Then she had an opportunity to teach in the district of Normadin, near Lake St. John (Lac St. Jean) in northern Quebec. It is likely that the workload in that part of the province was lighter and therefore more enjoyable. Instructions in both languages (English and French) were not compulsory at the time, evidently. It is only recently that students in that locality have been given an opportunity to learn the English language and thus to become bilingual. This was indeed very deplorable as the Quebecois of today lament the fact that they have been deprived, (to their detriment), of the advantages their western cousins enjoyed. It did, however, benefit and lighten the duties of the classroom teachers. Consequently, they were able to participate in the social life of the community and enjoy some leisure and recreational activities. Ensuing from these circumstances, my mother's memories of her sojourn in Normandin were pleasurable. Her many talents and contributions to community functions entitled her to a wide popularity. Her musical ability must have been cherished. To the Quebecois, a social gathering or festivity is not complete unless it includes playing various instruments. The singing of countless refrains interminably until the wee hours of the next morning also forms part of the festivities.

It was while she was teaching in the district of Normandin that my mother met and married my dad, Noël. Apparently, theirs was love at first sight. Whenever she told the story she always claimed that she knew at first glance that he was the man she would marry. At the time she was being courted by my Uncle George, dad's brother. The couple had been invited to a family wedding. While waiting for the guests to assemble, my dad came down from the upstairs, dressed in wedding attire. "As soon as I saw him," she declared years afterwards, "I knew then and there that there would never by anyone else in my life." An enduring love it was, unquestionably, to have come through the rigors of pioneer days, the destitution of the dirty thirties, raising a family on nihility (zilch) and surviving.

What made the success of this marriage so astonishing was, (besides all the exterior alien factors), the incompatibility of their characters and the conflict of their aspirations. Yet amidst all the harsh struggles they encountered, neither of them ever admitted regretting their union. Perhaps there is some truth in the trite cliché that love conquers all!

My mother had been given every opportunity to reach her potential and self-fulfillment. Elite educational facilities, training in the arts, and music, propriety in manners and comportment, had all been facets in her developmental background. Most significant of all, her parent's valued education as the most crucial factor in the raising and nurturing of their children. Although he was a very intelligent man, my father never had these opportunities. At a very early age, he became instrumental in providing the needs of a large family. He worked in a textile factory (probably in the States). According to my research, child labor laws had yet to be implemented and enforced. The children were compelled to work long hours in one shift. Compulsory education was also yet to be implemented. It appears that both the government in Canada and the States vacillated on this point because the economical contributions of the offspring were crucial to the support of the household.

It is obvious that these two individuals, directed towards opposite orientation, would differ in their holistic approach towards life. One embarking on life's journey with an artistic, creative and professional approach, while the other, with a more practical view, the belief that providing the means essential to survival predominated over all other objectives.

For some time after they were married my parents lived in Montreal. My dad worked as a longshoreman. My mother was not teaching, her time being completely devoted to the care of her children. My brothers Jean, George, and my sister Yvonne, were born in that great city.

Somehow the vibes trickling through the years whisper incessantly the words that were never spoken audibly. It is the cry of one torn between the throes of a passionate love and an aching heart. The speculation of what lies secretly hidden beneath the ripple of those vibes is hazardous, but the compelling temptation to reveal them is irresistible.

Her career was abruptly reversed. Her role as a professional, the pursuit of knowledge and the arts was superseded by a role devoid of intellectual challenge. She became exclusively a mother and a housewife, which indeed is a noble and rewarding calling.

However, settled in a strange Montreal district, she had few close acquaintances and therefore longed for adult companionship. She was restricted to the care of the children and confined indoors. There was little opportunity or time for the pursuit of her obsessive intellectual and artistic passions. Surely she had access to her books, her beloved books! Without those she would certainly not have survived. Yet her intense love for her husband and children compensated for her loneliness, and the relinquishing all that was the very essence of her being - music, drama, literature, the arts, the nucleus of her existence. Without these she felt dispossessed and deprived of her vital and essential nature.

Surpassing all these, however, and perhaps the most distressing of her plight was my dad's continual absence. The rigorous labor's exigencies, compounded by the demands his co-workers imposed upon him, weighed heavily on my dad's daily schedule. Consequently my mother was left alone, single-handedly to contend with the trauma of being transplanted into a laborer's world, unfamiliar to her, besides being solely responsible for the care of three infants.

The sheltered convent life followed by the esteemed position as a teacher was incompatible and conflicted irreconcilably to the role that now confronted her. She had forsaken the pursuit of the arts, her independent economic status, her social life and was faced with the astronomical task of caring for three young children.

On the other hand, my dad also found himself in an untenable, impossible situation. As a longshoreman he felt compelled to become one of the group. In other words he wanted to be accepted by his co-workers. In some situations, becoming a member of the crowd can be precarious, and the consequences can have unpredictable repercussions. These may be especially disastrous, contingent upon certain stipulations or predicaments that exist in the world of employment, both in the fields of professional and trade.

Subsequent to the above, I have made an observation that is especially relevant in the field of trades people. Although it may reek of stereotyping, it is not my intention to categorize. The very word itself is repugnant to me. It is rather my desire, in many instances, to praise or vindicate, rather than incriminate. The brutal exigencies labor imposes on their physical and mental faculties tends to make the workers feel oppressed and that they are being exploited (justifiably so, in many instances). They feel that they deserve compensations for their grueling exertions. As a result, many, after their shift, instead of going straight home to their families, stop at the local pub with the rest of the boys, for a beer (or beers?). As a tradesman it is hazardous not to conform to the group's norms. Anyone who dares stand apart is considered odd or even weird. His job is often at stake. Not many have the courage to resist the temptation to be swept with the tide. Unfortunately my dad was caught up in this vicious trend and became imbued in its cult with disastrous repercussions.

To those who are involved, it often appears impossible to disengage themselves from a hopeless situation. The issues entailed are so complicated, so crucial, that any course of action appears futile. In other words there seems to be no way out of the dilemma. And that was the situation confronting my parents as they visualized it. It was imperative that decisive and immediate action had to be taken in order to solve the crisis. There seemed to be only one alternative, although it proved to be temporary. The family decided to move near Lac St. Jean, Quebec, where the grandparents lived.

It was a mixed farming community - dairying, grain cultivation, etc. Most of my dad's brothers and sisters were established on small farms of their own. Subsequently, my dad was granted a homestead, and looked forward to building a home for his family. The immediate and urgent problems had been left behind and a new, more desirable future anticipated.

Although the move solved some of the more urgent problems, it was not a permanent solution. Many other concerns had to be addressed and dealt with in the immediate future. Perhaps the most crucial of these was the matter of economics.

The land that had been granted to my dad was unproductive, mostly sand. It was at the time not cultivated. My mother's time was devoted to the care of the children. The prospects for securing a reliable source of income were grim. It is probable that my dad's expertise in the forest industry was their only recourse. The products from the luxurious forests yielded an income barely sufficient for the needs of his family.

Though they were in the midst of relatives and friends, other concerns continually emerged. It is true that being in a familiar milieu, they felt the blessing of security and well being emanating from friendship and good neighbors.

The social aspect brought many repercussions. After the loneliness she had experienced in Montreal, my mother thrived on the friendly adult relationship. Having someone to converse with and to share your feelings and aspirations must have been a little bit of paradise.

There was also a negative side to the social aspect. The family reunion brought great happiness to all its members. The rejoicing and celebrations never ceased. One party followed another with songs, dancing and revelry. The rippling of the vibes tells me that this celebrating may have been too strenuous for my mother. With three children the partying is over.

The cabin in which they lived had been a temporary shelter for the grandparents, while the permanent family residence had been constructed. It stood in the valley at the foot of a hill. It was a very small cabin, yet it provided for the urgent and immediate shelter required by the family.

My brother has a flash recollection of an incident that occurred in that cabin. This quotation is an exact replica of the words he used when he related the experience to me: "I lean over the half-door and the picture of a woman, my mother, flashes, clearly framed, into my consciousness. The image is crystal clear. She is seated on a rocking chair. There is a child standing close beside her, and another, an infant, upon her lap. Although only about four years old, the scene will, as it flashes back distinctly before my eyes, follow me the rest of my days."

Jean has vivid memories of the cabin itself, and the hill below which it stood. An older cousin, still living in the vicinity, testifies that my brother had, from his childhood memories, given an exact description of the cabin and the site where it was situated.

Although the cabin itself has long since vanished, the permanent residence, where the grandparents lived, still stands, in immaculate condition, a living proof of the family heritage. This cousin, Henri, referred to above, remembers watching Jean trudging awkwardly behind his dad, as the two of them were making their way to the homestead to prepare the land for cultivation.

There are so many memories...so many stories...some of which Jean and the three of us were actually fortunate enough, as we visited our relatives in Quebec, to observe first hand. The joy emanating from the acquaintance with our first cousins was an unforgettable experience. Guided and accompanied by these resident cousins, we visited many of the places our parents had constantly mentioned. The priory, or priests retirement home, was constructed under the auspices of my cousin, the Abbey, and stands prominently, majestically, on top of a hill.

There is a large track of land in the vicinity of the lake which abounds in blueberries. It is owned by several of the local people who have named it l'Afrique. The blueberries are so plentiful that the sale of the fruit has been converted into a commercial enterprise. When the blueberry season rolls around, all other activities are abandoned temporarily. Picking, cleaning, packaging, and selling the fruit become a priority. The packaging takes place in a small shelter in the middle of each owner's field. Twenty-four small plastic baskets weighing approximately one hundred grams are placed in a large wooden crate. The crates are then sold to local merchants. It is, apparently, a most lucrative enterprise. The proceeds are not sufficient to support a family for a year or until the next season, but it immensely replenishes the family's dwindling budget. All local people are very proud of this valuable natural resource.

FATHER'S STORY

Vivid images of my father keep flashing before my eyes. I see him distinctly; evenings, smoking his pipe in his favorite rocking chair, exalting in the trance his suspense filled tales have cast upon his transfixed enchanted audience. For he was a great storyteller! He told tales - thrillers - that sent chills up and down your spine - mysteries, comedies, and true life experiences. Many times he was joined by his friend, Mr. Roger Beautemps, whose expertise at spinning a yarn was unparallel. The two of them had a knack for story telling that held their audiences mesmerized, spellbound, or in stitches with laughter. Many evenings were spent sitting around the fire, fascinated, listening to these exciting "contes" told by these two expert storytellers. At times my mother joined them. Her stories always emanated from the infinite number of books she had read and usually were not true life experiences.

Some of these "contes" were in some way a typical reflection on the French Canadian culture. They cast a glimpse upon the lifestyle and temperament of the Quebecois in the 19th century. They portrayed the special qualities and characteristics that made and makes the Quebecois unique, outstanding and distinct.

Other tales were derived from my dad's true life experiences. These were especially intriguing. Many of them concerned real live encounters with famous celebrities. Others were of famous attractions like the "Barnum and Bailey Circus". Most of these occurred while my dad worked in various states south of the border, and in southeastern Quebec.

These were happy times, full of laughter, and the enjoyment and security of being together!

From the many chronicles and narratives emanating from his memoirs, it is undeniably evident that my dad's happiest years were those in which he lived in the States. His parents must have moved south when he was a very young lad. From the way he spoke, he worked in the textile factories when he was yet very young. He spoke with pride of winning the favor of the superintendents. His skills, dexterity and speed while spinning and weaving fibers into cloth, using complicated machines were remarkable. It was an enjoyable part of his life.

From the textile factories he was employed for many years in the lumber industry. He mentioned several locations, but the state which kept recurring in his recitals was "Connecticut". He may have been there for a longer period of time or perhaps he liked that state best.

But what was unmistakably clear was his enamoured memories of those years. You could hear it in his voice. You could feel the vibes throbbing in his heart, longing for the life he had left behind and knowing that it was gone forever.

He loved the regular schedules of the lumber camp, the orderly, clean surroundings. He loved the security of doing a day's work for a day's wage, versus the uncertainty and risk involved in farming. The leisure hours filled with contests of strength and the interminable hours spinning yarns delighted my dad. He undoubtedly could tell a yarn with the best of them.

Besides all these benefits was the excellence of the meals, especially the luscious and scrumptious pies. No earthly being could even dream of baking a pie as delicious and with such a flaky crust. According to my dad, camp life was the ultimate. There was never any mention or complaints of backbreaking labor, of the long shifts, or of the fatigue. The comfort he felt in the well ordered, undeviating regular routine of the lumber camp was a reflection and clearly illustrated my dad's character and personality.

It undeniably demonstrated the man's tireless and industrious nature. It also exhibited his obsession for order and punctuality. His abhorrence for indolence, disorganization and confusion was inordinate. His love for organization and order manifested itself in everything he did. His shop was arranged in a specific order. Every tool hung in its particular hook, where it could be found when needed. The irresponsibility of failing to replace a tool in its proper place was beyond his comprehension. Thus when he found his shop in confusion he became exceedingly irritated. The repercussions were at times highly turbulent, shattering the tranquility of the still waters.

When his parents decided to return to Quebec, they settled near Lake St. John (Lac St. Jean) in the county of Normandin. Other members of the family settled in St. Felician, Chicoutimi, and St. Thomas Didyme. Most members were adults and some were already married. Each family was granted a track of land and planned to establish a home in the vicinity. Being the second youngest in the family, my father was yet a young man and was single before he met my mother. He had not prepared his land for cultivation or built a home of his own. Nonetheless, he had doubtlessly intended to settle among his people, his family, friends, and relatives. Being established in the midst of his own people, his own culture and language provided my dad with the stability and security so crucial to his happiness and well being. Although he had reluctantly reconciled himself to the departure from the States and submitted to the resettlement in Quebec, he found compensation being with his own people.

When he was confronted with the suggestion of relocating in the west he was appalled. He had just resigned himself to a new way of life and could not envision readapting in an uncertain and hostile environment. He passionately opposed the venture and resisted it at great lengths. It may have been the propaganda, the dream of a better way of life, or perhaps my mother's persuasion, but at last he yielded. Like many others he embarked on the great exodus to the west.

Is it any wonder that a man with such a temperament felt displaced, utterly disoriented in a strange new environment. A land that threatened his and the survival of his family, where the future was uncertain, yet challenging. Is it any wonder that the rationality of this relocation was questioned.

It is undeniably true that not only my father but many abandoned every aspect of life as they knew it. They left homes, their native habitat, the only familiar milieu and cultural background they had known. Their families and friends were left behind. They were cast into a pioneering situation completely foreign to them. They were confronted by forests, land as yet untouched by human hands. The task of establishing a home in such harsh circumstances was excruciating.

The exigency of preparing the soil for cultivation in an untamed wilderness and building a shelter for the family all at once must have been overwhelming indeed.

Most pioneers endured these hardships with patience. They had visualized this venture as the realization of a dream.

My father had not been fully convinced of the justifications and logic of this bold venture. Leaving the security of a well established home to embark into an uncertain, hazardous adventure disturbed him exceedingly. He was compelled or persuaded to acquiesce, nonetheless. But he never reconciled himself to the new situation. He reluctantly attempted to resign himself to the new way of life. But he longed with an aching heart for the home he had left behind. No other place would ever be home to him henceforth.

Besides feeling dislocated, my father was forced into an occupation that was entirely incompatible to him. Previously he had been employed in the lumber industry and was unprepared for the task of cultivating the land. He had loved working in the woods, surrounded by the beauty and freedom of nature. He knew and could identify every tree, every bird. He loved the wild animals and enjoyed watching and learning their habits.

On the farm he felt confined. He envisioned the fence enclosing his land as the prison bars, the barricade that held him captive. Nonetheless he endured his captivity but always longing for the freedom he had forfeited. He remained on the premises, constantly laboring at the unrewarding, unpredictable task of cultivating the land.

He had surrendered to his captivity irrevocably, obviously! He refused to leave the house for any pretext or occasion. It was very rare indeed that he could be persuaded to visit neighbors or friends for an evening. He always found a sensible reason or excuse to stay home.

The strenuous and constant labor that is involved in farming was not the problem. My father was a tireless, indefatigable laborer. His employers constantly praised his skill and the productivity of his work. It was rather the ability to manage the business of farming that was problematic. Although the soil on his homestead was the most fertile and productive in the area, our family was perhaps the most impoverished of the whole neighbourhood. Many blamed my father's love for the horses and determination to cater to them, treating them as pets rather than workers for this situation. Nonetheless for one reason or another, the land failed to yield the profits necessary to provide a livelihood for the family.

It is most tragic that many times human beings do not become cognizant of the truth before it is too late. What is even more tragic is that many go to their graves without ever enjoying the solace, the assuagement of the understanding that is always subsequent to enlightenment.

It was many long years after his demise that I finally began to understand and sympathize with my father's predicament and discontent. It took endless speculation before I could assemble and weigh the interwoven events that had been directly accountable for his dismal attitude.

It is regretfully too late to apologize and make amends for the lack of understanding and misguided condemnation that many still harbor in some hearts. Words do not erase or ease the anguish that constantly consumes them. Most of the family members still insist that my dad was difficult. "He was impossible" they claim, "he made our childhood unbearable", others say, "I have no fond memories of my childhood."

Tears, painful memories, walking endlessly in the woods for comfort, yes those are painful recollections. But unbearable? Never! There were too many other times, joyful happy times that compensated for the times of stress.

Yet the one who in an effort to vindicate someone's inexplicable behavior, behavior that caused so much pain, may be the one who took the wrong turn at the crossroads. So perhaps it takes many long years for truth and justice to be recognized. People say that you don't see the truth until it hits you in the face. How true! Perhaps my dad's incessant grumbling and bitching was a protest against the fact that he was confronted with one crisis after another in adverse and alien circumstances. One whose protests were disregarded - no one heard or paid any attention to them.

Yet, I cannot but feel compassion for someone who although disinclined, struggled to the utmost of his ability in a valorous effort just to carry on in an untenable situation.

WESTWARD HO!

In 1913 my parents, with three of their children, came to join my grandparents Savard on the vast and fertile prairies of the west. The compelling force that could impel...lure these (and many others) courageous people to leave their loved ones, their homes, friends and everything they had ever known, to face the insecurity, the grueling hardships, deprivations, loneliness, constant labor and trials of pioneer life is almost incomprehensible. This mystifying enigma is indeed the ultimate in complexity. The reasons for the departure were numerous, and varied with each individual household. They were, oftentimes, very personal. However, most were following a dream, the dream of a more prosperous future and a more luxurious standard of living. There is no doubt, nonetheless, that the government was an impelling force, exerting great pressure, a veritable <u>push</u> and was unquestionably instrumental in the outcome of the final decision. This cyclopean exodus, this feverish agitation was the direct consequence and subsequent to the government's determination to fulfill an objective of colossal enormity.

In the later part of the 19th and the beginning of the 20th century the government of Canada became deeply concerned and preoccupied regarding the development and settlement of the west. Its crucial impact on the future of the nation was seriously considered. The matter was thoroughly investigated and the most practical method of accomplishing such a formidable task meticulously deliberated.

In order to achieve this goal several sequential measures or modus operandi were set in motion.

In the year 1885 a transcontinental railway was completed facilitating transportation of goods and passengers. It also obviously provided communication between the east and west.

Then the government launched an enormous campaign in an attempt to encourage immigration to the undeveloped virgin land. In order to achieve their goal, government officials used forceful, impelling and persuasive means to advertise the benefits and the advantages of resettlement. Newspapers, notices, bulletin boards, and placards were swarming with the praises of the western world. It was depicted as a land of plenty, where not only the streets but the very fields were paved with gold. A veritable Garden of Eden. These beguiling promises of a more attractive future and the means of improving their living standard lured many to the new land. The move was advertised as a golden opportunity as a large track of free land was granted to each settler (then it comprised 160 acres). This piece of land was known as the settler's homestead.

It is little wonder that not only my parents, but thousands were lured into the venture. Countless eastern Canadians were convinced of the compelling western attraction. They were not alone. The compelling and forceful propaganda also brought thousands of Europeans to settle in western Canada.

This intensive, compelling promotion wasn't the sole reason why my parents came west. My grandfather, grandmother and the younger members of the family were already well established on their homestead. Communications from them created favorable impressions on the quality of life they enjoyed. These reports and the desire to have a close relationship with my grandparents had a major impact on my parents' decision. The most decisive unquestionable motive, however, was too personal, too sensitive, and confidential to relate without being disloyal to family traditions.

There are people in Quebec who resent those who left "la belle province". They "le Quebecois" feel betrayed by the departure of their fellow citizens who have abandoned them and thus broken the bonds that held them together as brothers. Those who remain have forsaken the wanderers. In fact, some of these people, in one fell swoop, have washed their hands permanently of both their relatives and their country. The country that they have discovered, founded, and nurtured. It is beyond all comprehension! The Quebecois knows that Canada is a masterpiece that he and others have created. As the master artisan of a "chef d'oeuvre" he should not cast it to the winds, but cherish and share its magnificence with others.

Had the Quebecois understood the traumatic ramifications of that formidable decision, the decision to move west, they would never have condemned those who pursued an irresistible, alluring dream. They would have understood that a colossal, impelling reason had incited it. It was and is a great consolation that this attitude was, and is not, shared by all of our brothers in "la belle province".

The heartache, the anguish, these brave adventurers must have endured in the final decisive implementation of their project is unfathomable. They must have been apprehensive indeed of the insecurity in confronting the unknown. They had to leave the only home they had ever known, their only friends, the only place where their foot seemed firmly planted upon familiar soil. They sold their homes and everything they owned. Filled with joyful anticipation, they embarked on the journey west.

At the time, travel across Canada was a major calamity! The only available means of transportation was the train. These were slow and failed to provide the necessary comforts of modern locomotives. Passengers traveling with children found the journey especially exhausting. My parents had three small children under the age of four. My older brother, aged three at the time, recalls (amazingly) having the time of his life running up and down the aisle on the train.

The train journey, however, was not the most grueling and strenuous hardship they endured during the trip. Railroad companies had yet to lay rails to connect all points in the new territory. Therefore, the remaining distance had to be traversed in a horse drawn vehicle. Many traveled in a wagon, a vehicle so rough it jarred every bone in the body. Yet, undaunted, these courageous people continued on their venture and succeeded in paving the way for future generations.

And there, at the journey's end, their trials had just begun. The most urgent exigency was the provision of an immediate shelter for the family. Many built makeshift log houses as temporary shelters. They intended to build better lumber homes in the future. Most did, but many others took refuge with relatives who had preceded them west.

That is precisely what my parents did. They stayed at my grandparents until suitable lodgings could be procured. Although this arrangement was supposed to be only temporary, it extended (stretched) into a whole year before the family home was constructed. At last, a log house was built on the family homestead. It was, presumably, to be replaced in the future by a more elaborate and comfortable building. For some obscure reason this replacement never did occur. The family continued to reside in this log structure until all of the members left and were on their own. This was a great disappointment to my mother, whose yearning frequently was reiterated, "all I want is a congenial and comfortable home" she sighed despairingly.

Decorum was to my father insignificant. He was content with the status quo, therefore he could not understand the urgency of improving the dwelling.

What was a woman of this caliber doing in this wilderness? One may justifiably wonder. A wilderness where mere survival was the crucial issue and where procuring a living from undeveloped, virgin land in deprived circumstances was an ordeal. A woman whose spirit dwelt in the unfathomable rapture inherent in literature, music and drama. A woman whose liberated spirit yearned for the mysticism that transcends all unrelenting reality.

Granted it was a land of promise. But only for those who had a close affinity to the soil and who felt a sense of belonging to it. Those who felt content to wrest the riches abiding in the bounteous gifts so lavish in the benevolence of Mother Earth. For those brave souls the land provided all the necessities of life. They built comfortable homes in later years, and some even became moderately well to do. Their dreams had been fulfilled and they were content. The west had provided the goal they had been seeking.

This was not the case with either of my parents. They had been lured into this venture by the beguiling promises of a more attractive future, and as a means of improving their standard of living. They found themselves in a wilderness. A land entirely alien to both their aspirations, capabilities and aptitudes. An environment that was absolutely incompatible to both of them. Emerging from metropolis like Montreal, they must have felt as if they had been suddenly ousted into a void, a land of emptiness, desolation and want. Alone with nature, their companions, the birds and the trees.

It was especially difficult for my father, who longed for distant horizons. He yearned for the organization, the well planned work schedules of industrial managements. He yearned for the recreational facilities he had previously enjoyed. Not only was he in a location that he disliked intensely, but he was forced to perform a labor that he detested and for which he lacked the necessary skills. Besides all this he and all the pioneers were forced to create, out of nullity (from scratch), their own destiny and provide for their own basic needs; lacking tools, machinery, equipment, and funds to purchase them. Their predicament had a close affinity to that of the cave man. From his own resourcefulness, ingenuity and cunning, this self-sufficient aboriginal provided, unaided, for his own needs. But at least this primitive man had an advantage. He had never experienced or known the luxury of modern civilization. He had never envisioned the rapture, the ecstasy of music, drama, literature, and all the arts. Therefore he was content when his hunger was satiated, protected from dangerous animals and sheltered from the unpredictable harshness of weather. It was not so with these émigré. They longed for the genre of life they feared could never be recaptured, and was lost forever.

Eventually most pioneers were able to provide for the immediate, if not luxurious, needs of their families. Each settler used his own ingenuity and special talents or skills to survive in a hostile environment. Some, who understood the problematic techniques of farming and the mysterious secrets of reaping the abundance abiding in the soil, became fairly affluent. They built comfortable homes, wore quality and stylish clothes, and enjoyed the benefits of their labor. They retained their culture, their language and religious traditions. Honest, honorable, industrious and worthy they were indeed, content in their new well established settlement. Nonetheless, in spite of their charitable, compassionate nature, they were unable to comprehend how anyone could justifiably be unable to enjoy the fruit of his own labor, or how circumstances could prevent the realization of a decent standard of living when prosperity was within their reach.

As a child I read a story entitled "One Man's Meat Is Another Man's Poison". Although the source and the author of this tale have long been forgotten, its psychological truth is irrefutable. While the soil was a source of plenitude and abundance to the other settlers, it was the source of bitter disappointment to both my parents. It was not the land of promise, but the land of desolation.

Neither of my parents were farmers (that's an understatement), especially my father. Wresting a living from the soil was not his calling. He loved animals too passionately. He was unable to force them into productivity. His heart was in the magic of the forest, the untamable wonders of nature.

HOME IN SASKATCHEWAN

I have long left far behind the confusion, the hurts, the deprivations and sadness of my childhood. But the mystic, the wonder of those childhood days still unshakably linger on within me.

The low, rugged, hilly mountains just beyond the barbed wire fence, the myriad sloughs all surrounded by tall grass, the tall pines towering above the swamps - swamps replete with cranberries, the joys derived from picking saskatoons, strawberries, blueberries...the expanse of uninhabited fields where one could wander aimlessly when filled with sadness or to escape from chaos. The laughter, the songs, the legends still ring in my ears, clearly, and I still join mystically those musical extravaganzas and wild frolic of the dances.

These cherished memoirs walk with me every step of the way on this hectic tortuous journey, wherever the caprice of destiny may choose to lure my path. It was with a deep longing to recapture and relive the wonders of those euphoric days that I set out to visit the scene where all these experiences, recollections had emanated. But I was totally unprepared for the bleak panorama that stretched indefinitely before my eyes. I was overwhelmed by the barren desolation nature's ravages had wrought. It felt as if our whole life had been suddenly, ruthlessly plucked from under our feet and that our existence had been a mere fantasy. As Shakespeare would say "the stuff that dreams are made of."

Nothing! Absolutely nothing! No trace to witness that this has been the site where a family's existence, emotions, joys pulsated, or where an intense struggle for survival ensued! Not a trace to mark the enactment of the vital performance played by its members! How complete and cruelly nature has obliterated with its beauteous mantel of greenery any sign of human existence! No sign of the log house, the barn, the tool shed or the blacksmith shop; not even of the milk house! A search for the turkey shed, built of bark laths, proves futile. Even the remains of the well, below the hill, had vanished. Yet the lofty poplar trees that surrounded it still stand jealously guarding its spot and arrogantly flourishing, displaying the branches on which the young recklessly climbed to the very top. The shuddering, shrieking echo of the spectral breeze plaintively lamenting the horror, the exasperation of the despairing father.

But this cannot be! The forsaken emptiness, the sadness, the desolation must be an illusion. For there, at the far end of the potato patch, still stand the tall imposing pines, as stately imperious as ever. There also dwells the remains of the lake, now dried and unassuming, that played so vital a role in sustaining the lives of those who seem to have vanished or never existed. The chokecherry trees flourish yet, the excessive weight of the abounding fruit bending and straining downward the branches upon which they so luxuriously grow. Other varieties of trees; pine, poplar, saskatoons, birch, willow, etc. cover with vengeance any trace of evidence where enacted a human panorama. The only relic that can attest or authenticate human habitation is a measly, pathetic jar of Pond's cold cream. What mockery! The ancient Egyptian's existence has been written in the layers of the earth. But we who lived and left but some recent years have been ruthlessly and relentlessly obliterated by the grim but magnificent splendor of nature's mantel.

Was it nature's farcical chicanery to beautifully drape that precious episode, the drama of our existence with its mantel of forgetfulness, indelible memorial of the impermanence of our existence there? What transience when lived was a microcosm of human experience, now lay beneath a canopy, camouflaged with green forgetfulness!

The search for the site where the house stood was heartbreaking. There was no evidence whatsoever that any kind of building ever stood where it should have been situated. Its remains exist only in the treasured memory of those to whom it was "home".

Le coupage de la glace en 1924
pour mettre dans les glaciers.
George et Noel Gaumond,
Napoleon Girouiard ,
cheveux Dan et Kate.

Sawing firewood on the Gaumond farm
SE.Sec 24.T 51.R 8.W.3rd.1927
There was no chain saw at that time

Four walls of hued logs formed the frame, the crevices plastered with clay. The second storey was framed in lumber, whitewashed regularly with lime. This spacious room served as a bedroom for the whole family. In the center of the ceiling a trap door opened up to access an attic, a makeshift storage and hiding place for the more adventurous and daring members of the family. The main floor, one large all-inclusive room, served as kitchen, dining room and living room. As you entered, facing the far wall, there was a wood stove in the right hand corner, a shelf above the stove was where all the spices were kept. Next to this stove and a few feet away from it was an "armoire" where all the linen and family clothing was meticulously piled and above this "armoire" were the law books. Huge, cumbersome volumes, ranging and leaning upright alternatively from one to thirteen, against the chimney. For lack of a more suitable space, there were also many musical instruments deposited "hit and miss" on this armoire. Besides all these there was the famous "medicine bag" filled with dry herbs and forever threatening to descend on any unsuspecting victim. Next to the armoire was the organ, piled high with countless musical instruments. Over the organ and beautifully framed hung a picture of my oldest brother Jean. The left wall was occupied by cupboards, a breadbox, then and a china cabinet. This china cabinet had been artistically fashioned by a skillful neighbor with a pocketknife. It was indeed a masterpiece. My dad's violin hung on the wall on its left. There was also a religious picture hanging on that wall on the left side of the window. At the foot of the stairs was a long homemade table. It was covered with oilcloth and flanked on either side by two long benches, also homemade. On the wall, behind the table hung the family clock. The staircase (under which the firewood was piled) led to the family's main upstairs bedroom. The entrance and access to this upstairs bedroom was flanked by a huge trap door which could be opened or closed as desired. It was usually used to hang items of clothing. To a child's overactive imagination, the fur coats hanging there often appeared as fierce forest beasts.

Books and musical instruments were a priority in that humble home. They were considered a necessity on par with food, clothing and shelter. The organ on the left hand corner of the log house was the most treasured item of the whole household. It was piled high with music books and music sheets on top of which were three violins (the violin hanging on the wall was my dad's and no one dared touch it). The other instruments; a guitar, an accordion, a xylophone, a ukulele, and several mouth organs, were wherever there was room available. It was indeed amazing that there was room for all of these! Perhaps some shared the space with the famous law books on top of the "armoire" that stood beside the organ. Who knows! These musical instruments and books were deeply cherished by the whole family and even by the friends who dropped in intermittently at their own pleasure and convenience. They (the instruments) brought infinite hours of happiness and ecstatic joy to all, especially to those who participated in the revelry of the improvised concerts.

In a home deprived of material wealth, luxury, and whose possessions comprised only the barest necessities, existed an intrinsic wealth surpassing all these in value. Music, books and love. Upon these my mother built the foundation of her domain. She reigned over it with a song, a story, love, and a word of wisdom.

As previously stated, my father was perfectly content to live in the mud plastered log house, or had he completely given up? He saw no need for improvement apparently! That was of course a great disappointment for my mother. And there in that log house the family remained until it was abandoned. It was kept immaculately clean. Every week the wood floor was scrubbed white until the boards were worn thin. The many windows were washed until the glass seemed to have disappeared. The cupboards, kitchen, armoire and clothes were cleaned every week. The care and reverence lavished upon this humble residence was on par or perhaps surpassed that conferred upon the queen's palace.

Indeed, to those who dwelt in it, it was their castle, their home! The log mud plastered walls, the lack of privacy and luxury did not impinge upon their happiness. All these denuded circumstances were envisioned as a matter of course. There were no reproaches, no self pity! The piano, all the musical instruments, the portraits, and the books more than compensated for all that was lacking. Perhaps the books were the most precious of all. There were books, books, and more books. Books in both languages, French and English. History books, law books, geography books, and most cherished of all, the novels. When all these had been read by all some were borrowed from the school (the school had an extensive library). Then when we ran out of these a traveling library was ordered. This library was a service provided by the government. It was crated in a large wooden box approximately 3 feet x 3 feet x 3 feet, and completely filled with books on diverse subjects. My mother read all the books contained in one box (crate) in a month and requested another.

Although books were cherished in our house, music was the ultimate treasure. The precious moments of rapture its melodious enchantment brought transcended all. It was what rallied the family together. It was what attracted friends and neighbors to our home. It is incomprehensible and utterly mysterious how my parents managed to purchase an organ without funds. But sure enough there it stood beaming proudly, in the most prestigious corner of the house. It was by no means isolated or unaccompanied. The truth is there were musical instruments strewn everywhere. They filled the whole house! An organ, three or four violins, a guitar, an accordion, a ukulele, a xylophone, and several harmonicas. A veritable orchestra. And that was besides the instruments musicians brought when they came to join our jovial concerts.

These musical extravaganzas were the ultimate in delight. Everyone present joined the merrymaking: family, friends, neighbors (even the dogs), musically inclined or not. Those who couldn't play an instrument either sang along or danced. It was fun!

My mother had taught the theory of music to everyone in the household. Therefore most of us could read music, but many could also play by ear. Both Marie Anne and Raymond had inherited my mother's uncanny musical talent and both sang like nightingales, besides playing every instrument within their reach.

She had also taught harmony. The violins played the compositions in three parts. One violinist played the melody while the other two violins played the harmony. The whole arrangement was accompanied on the organ and guitar. A regular band, no less! Whenever it was possible and appropriate, the whole concert was complemented by those who sang the lyrical content of the piece being performed. These vocalists also harmonized singing in the different parts - the bass, the alto and the soprano. It was usually the young people who provided the vocal contributions to the makeshift concerts. In my mind's eye there is a vivid recollection of the local teacher (a dear charming lady) singing "Joan of Arc" (in French) accompanied and directed by the organist. There were many others who possessed melodious voices and who came just to join in the choral group for pure enjoyment and fun.

Those who played instruments also assembled at our place. Although most of those players lacked instructions on musical theory and played by ear, their interpretations were impeccable, extraordinary! They never strayed from the true harmonious rendition of the melody. One of the regular violinists, a very special friend, played for hours to the accompaniment of the organ or guitar. Pure enjoyment and ecstasy emanated from his endless repertoire of refrains, or tunes as he called them. Needless to say, he was uncommonly popular with everyone, especially at the amusement and recreation hall, where he played for local dances.

Thus from this musical and dramatic atmosphere emanated the fact that the house was forever packed with people, young and old. The young came to sing, dance and socialize. They simply wanted to have fun. The older and more mature guests came to enjoy good conversation or play a game of cards. Some needed moral support. Perhaps the uncomplicated aura of the home provided a reprieve from the daily grind of farm work and family problems. Needless to say many came for other than recreational reasons.

It was from this humble refuge that a prodigious, indomitable family emanated. It was from that same refuge that each member set out on the complicated, eventful journey of life. It was a retreat deprived of means but not of riches - deprived of wealth but not of treasures. It was also there in that same shelter that the members shared their joys, their laughter, and their tears.

It is my intent to cast but a brief glimpse into the lives of each living member of that remarkable household. A glimpse as they were before the world had laid its mark on them or claimed them for its own.

There were eleven in the family. Actually there were fourteen but three died in infancy. Paul Emil died during the Spanish Flu and one was born ill. Gerard, at twenty months, died from pneumonia. A doctor was unavailable and the home remedies were not potent enough to save him.

Jean was the oldest. He was a no-nonsense guy. From his earliest years, he had decided that when something needed to be done it was done, no procrastinating! At three he trudged awkwardly along behind his father on the way to prepare the land for cultivation. At ten during harvest he decided that he could steer the horses pulling the binder that cut the wheat. So he begged and he pleaded. Both my parents thought it was too dangerous. So Jean followed behind the binder, up and down the field, down and up the field. No amount of persuasion or fatigue could dissuade him. At last, in desperation, my dad thought, "I may as well let him ride. At least he won't get so tired". So Jean sat on the seat of the binder, proud as a peacock and held the reins guiding the horses. Soon that wasn't good enough. The chant "Let me do it by myself. I can do it. Let me try," went on and on. So my dad thought, "He's doing so well. I'll be right behind him. I'll let him go around the field and watch him closely." He did so well that he cut all the wheat and other crops by himself with my dad following very closely behind, watching, and stooking the sheaves. Both father and son were bursting with pride as they related their achievement. "We did it together, Dad and I. We harvested the whole crop together." It was the same story coming from the proud father. "He drove these horses like an expert. I am amazed that such a young lad could perform a task for the first time as if he had been doing it all his life," he would boast, beaming with pride.

Cutting wheat crop in 1932 on Gaumond farm SE-S 24 T-51 R-8,W-3rd,two binder,

Jean was methodical and reliable. Every venture was undertaken with zealous dedication when he was in charge. Incompetency and inefficiency were intolerable and incomprehensible to him. He expected excellence, punctuality and organization in every venture and activity.

This wholehearted approach manifested itself in all forms of diversion and entertainment. He loved partying and having fun. Usually he was the life of the festivities, being very popular and outgoing. At dances he was the "caller" for the old fashioned quadrilles.

There are several incidences in my older brother Jean's eventful life that are most electrifying. One of these happened when he was home for Christmas and is related below in his own words.

"I was twenty-one. Mother and I had gone to Debden to do the Christmas shopping. We were on our way back, returning home through the bush, late at night. It was 40 below zero. We had just crossed the ravine when six timber wolves came out of the bushes. Two of them were on each side of our sleigh and two ahead. It was broad daylight because the moon was so bright. The timber wolves kept following us, stalking us at a distance for about a mile. The team of horses, Dan and Kate, were extremely nervous. They increased their speed. Their ears stood right up and neighed frantically. I asked mom if she was scared. "I don't like it," she replied, "Are you scared?" "I don't like it either!", was my reply. When we got into the clearing and civilization, the wolves dispersed. "We both breathed a profound sigh of relief."

Another dramatic event occurred in the year 1931, while the men were working as they did every winter, in the forest of northern Saskatchewan. 1931, that was the year that the earth got closer to the moon or vice versa. The incident is again narrated in John's own words.

"It was early December 1931. Our camp was situated one mile north of Deep Lake. We had gone to Big River with my Uncle Charles from our camp (a distance of approximately 18 miles) to get a 'tie permit'. We were using a team of horses with a sleigh and wagon box. By the time we had finished our business in town we were late coming back at night. One of us always stood in front of the box and one walked behind the sleigh to keep warm. It was my turn to ride in front of the box. I was watching and making sure that the horses were following the morning track as we had gone cross-country in the morning. Coming back about three miles north from the camp we were traveling an open swamp in a southeast direction at the time. Uncle as usual smoked his pipe as he walked along behind the sleigh. All at once I saw a big light. I thought that Uncle Charles was probably lighting his pipe, but as I turned my head I saw a huge, dazzling, bright red ball of fire creating and tracing a luminous trail above the tree line traveling in a northerly direction. It created such a glare that it illuminated the whole area. It kept going until it disappeared behind the tree line. When we first saw it, it was quite high. It lasted about a minute before it disappeared in a northwesterly direction behind the trees. Whether this bizarre event was related to the proximity of the moon remains speculative."

Men hauling fish at rabbit Hill 1927.
some name remember,Snell Omen,Ovila
Dore.Fred Doucette,Alec Mudrak,Burnuf,

At seventeen John joined the crews of freighters who transported fish from the northern lakes of Saskatchewan. These freighters brought supplies to the fish camps and took fish back to the shipping stations where it was shipped by rail to interested buyers. The fish camps were situated near the numerous lakes in the Canadian Northland. These lakes were teaming with fish. Many entrepreneurs envisioned this abundance of fish as a great business opportunity and hoped to build a great commercial fishing industry near the northern lakes. Many business enterprises were ventured by different men and partnerships. Some of these flourished at the beginning but were eventually unsuccessful. For many years there was a great deal of business activity in the commercial and shipping centers and this industry provided employment for many during the depression. It appears that single business traders were more successful than the large companies. John's memories of that episode not only manifest the perils, the hazards of the adventures, but also the excitement, the thrill of the exploits. The hardships that confronted these brave men were formidable. They traveled in an open sleigh that was equipped with a huge flat platform over the runners in temperatures ranging from -30 to -80. The distance from the shipping center to the fish camp was remote; sometimes from sixty to a hundred miles or more. That distance could not be covered in one day. Consequently it was necessary to camp (make camp it was called) several times along the way. Both the freighter and the horses had to be fed and rested in order to travel the rest of the journey. A fire had to be kept burning all night. If the men traveled in pairs, one man would keep the fire going while the other slept, in other words they took turns sleeping. But otherwise a freighter did not risk falling asleep less the fire went out. Without it he would most certainly have frozen to death.

Loads of fish on the beaver river north
Of Beauval in 1927.

At the camp the fish was packed in boxes. These were loaded
and stacked heavily on the sleigh's platform. The heavy load was pulled
by a team of horses. On the return journey the sleigh was loaded with
supplies for the fishermen.

Historically, the growth of commercial centers such as Big River, Prince Albert, Meadow Lake and Ile la Crosse (and many others) emanated directly from their strategic position. These cities were situated smack (right) in the interior of the country's most luxurious abundance of natural resources. In the early exploration and settlement of the West, during the thriving fur trade days, they were established as fur trading posts. But as the demand for furs began to dwindle and the commerce in this field was no longer lucrative it was replaced by the lumber and fishing industry. These centers were at the very core of the northern lakes teeming with fish and the luxurious forest. Consequently commercial businesses and trading activities converged at these focal points. These strategic points played an important role and were instrumental in the early development and opening of the Canadian West.

George was the second eldest in the family. He was the most compassionate, generous, thoughtful person that ever trod upon this earth. If only his spirit could hear the cry from all our hearts, as we sing out "thank you, thank you".... a million times over and over for his magnanimousity! Alas it is too late! He is beyond the realm of our call. For he never failed to come to our aid when the situation was critical and he thought we would be in trouble. He even offered to knead the bread or do whatever task to relieve the load in times of stress. How deeply, passionately everyone appreciated his generosity. Nonetheless it is debatable if anyone ever expressed that heart-felt gratitude. Regretfully it is too late! If we only could go back in time and rectify what we then failed to do.

What was most amazing, utterly inconsistent, was that when anything went wrong, anything at all (maybe even inclement weather), George was blamed for it. Even now I still hear the words ringing in my ears, "It's George's fault!" It never failed!

Poor George. He had a "homestead" some distance from where we lived. There was always some reason or excuse why he could not get the help he needed to cultivate it. The machinery, the horses were always unavailable! He probably lost the land as a result as the conditions or stipulations were that a certain amount of development on the land was to be completed each year for entitlement. George was never financially successful. He was too generous, too trusting! Someone always took advantage of his good nature. He even lost the girl of his dreams to someone less worthy but more outwardly flamboyant. However this story must be told in another context.

During the depression in the thirties, the labor situation had become desperate. The possibility of obtaining gainful employment was out of the question. In desperation my Uncle Armand, George and two cousins decided to seek employment in British Columbia. Not one of them had any money to cover the fare on the train, so they decided to venture the trip using an old "Model T" ford that had seen better days and should have been retired years before. It was an absolute wreck, a "beater" no less!!! It was a most hazardous decision. Gas money was all they had. In fact the whole enterprise was fraught with danger. It was unsafe to embark on such a long perilous journey without a reliable vehicle. Especially that the contentious old Model T they were using had a mind of its own. On level roads it ran like a queen, but it tenaciously, irrevocably, refused to climb hills. On the way they had it planned to a T. Whenever they saw an incline ahead all three boys would jump out automatically and push "her majesty" up to the top. It was a steady ritual. It also provided the group with a distraction. The old Model T was something to poke fun at. The boys insisted that they never had so much fun in their lives. They did, in spite of all the perils, reach their destination. What happened to the old contentious queen would be interesting to know. It could be the materials for another tale. The boys and Uncle did finally get work after experiencing many bitter disappointments.

It may be his gentle, benevolent nature that inspired Sleeping Beauty's fairies to generously bequeath some special gifts upon George. Above all, he was an artist. His artistic genius manifested itself almost from the cradle. What made this gift so extraordinary was the fact that George had very poor vision. Perhaps the beauty he could barely discern with his eyes, he envisioned and felt in his heart. His passion for beauty was revealed and expounded in all his artistic creations.

His most frequent subject was nature. He delighted portraying nature in its entire splendor. The mountains, lakes, the magic of the woods, the grandeur of the ocean, the vastness of the open prairie, the wild life, were all displayed with a unique quality of his own. He depicted wild animals fully alive, watchful, ready for sudden action, even appearing to leap out of the picture. One of his masterpieces was of a fawn coming out of a dense forest into a clearing. The fawn was vigilant, listening, watching for any sign of danger. The tension, uneasiness and apprehension were plainly manifested in the fawn's eyes and his whole composure. This picture was magnificent, exquisite!!!

Connoisseurs in the arts would have classified George's work as "realism". The drawings depicted the subject exactly as they appeared in reality.

George's talent was not confined exclusively to drawing and sketching. He had an uncanny skill in architecture – a skill which came natural to him. He had never been trained or even worked with carpenters in the trade. Nonetheless when a project was to be done, he visualized and designed its completion before it was even begun. This skill was greatly appreciated by my sister, Hélène. She needed an addition to her house. George planned and guided the whole operation. The result was perfect, even beyond all expectations.

He also made furniture such as medicine cabinets, bookcases, hope chests, from material he found in nature or from things discarded by others. For instance, he made a chest for Hélène that was unique. It was constructed with rare pieces of wood. The hinges and lock were constructed of bone. That chest proved to be his architectural masterpiece.

George's artistic gift enabled him to visualize how the furniture, the pictures, and ornaments should be arranged to create the best impression in a room. "It is utterly inconceivable that folks with luxurious furniture are unable to arrange them in a proper manner," he lamented.

George was unable to attend school for any length of time because my parents could not afford to get his eyes tested and buy him glasses. Yet, in spite of this obstacle, the fairies must have waved their magic wands indeed, because they granted George not one, but three gifts: the compassion of saints, the prodigious creativity of an artist, and the amazing skill of an architect.

It is extremely disturbing for me to talk about my oldest sister, Yvonne. Some of those memories abound in joy and happiness. Others are poignant with heartache and sadness.

As a consequence of her unpropitious and frail constitution, my mother was unable to assume the full responsibilities and management of the duties necessitated by the exigency of a large family. The ramifications of this predicament upon the older members of the family were prodigious. Especially on Yvonne, who was the eldest of the girls. Burdened with the care of the younger brothers and sisters and practically most of the household duties, she never experienced the normal mystical wonders, the magical world of childhood.

Her entire devotion to the children complemented her kind, affectionate nature and was a true manifestation of her love for them. She was truly like a second mother to the rest of the family. Meticulous, dedicated, she kept the humble home scrupulously clean; her impeccable organization and orderliness of the dwelling befitting and worthy of a palace.

She apparently assumed this role when she was very young. An incident occurred when she was four that set the stage and predicted the fate of her life at home in the future. She was dancing with the youngest child and accidentally dropped him/her. Too frightened and stunned to move, she just stood there and stared at the screaming child. "At least pick the child up" exhorted my mother. The amazing and most extraordinary thing about the role she had assumed seemed to be what was expected of her. And what was even more astounding was that she expected it of herself. She firmly believed that it was her duty sine qua non to perform all these tasks. My mother was extremely grateful to her and so was the rest of the family.

My dad did not seem to realize that what his daughter was doing was beyond the call of duty. It may be that it was traditional in his family that everyone irrevocably contributed to the welfare of all, or it may be that his personal problems were so overwhelming that he could feel no compassion whatsoever and was unable to empathize with someone else's distress. Or was it that the labor he performed was so brutal, exorbitant and excruciating that his exhaustion was beyond human endurance.

Oh, if only a person could have understood the trauma, the complexities that lay beyond those tragic episodes, their memories would have been less painful. Some past incidences are best left buried deeply fathoms below, there never to be unearthed. Yet they persistently, furtively, return, stalking, to haunt and torment the hitherto blissful remembrances. One of these regretful incidences happened years, many, many years ago when the whole family was still young and living at home. It was late at night and till then Yvonne had been rocking the youngest child who wouldn't settle down. Thinking that the child had at last mercifully gone to sleep she put him down. But alas! He let out a horrendous, ungodly wail that shook the whole house and woke everyone from their sleep. I will never forget my father's ferocious outrage. His abusing language, his threatening accusations, as he held her responsible for the child's capricious, overindulged nature. As usual my mother restored the peace, rebuking her husband for such a violent, unreasonable, unjustifiable burst of temper. Subsequently the poor girl must have, sleeplessly, rocked the child the remainder of the night, sobbing desperately and wondering hopelessly what atrocity she had supposedly committed. Hopefully these episodes were few and far between. The saying that misery breeds misery must be true! When people are tested beyond human endurance, they do things that are unpardonable, utterly inexcusable, which they regret bitterly for the rest of their lives.

Most of the memories associated with Yvonne are filled with warmth and happiness. Her affectionate, selfless, solicitous nature endeared her to all. In our home she gave the rest of the family the affection the parents were too preoccupied to give. She guided, consoled and counseled. She gave information, recommendations, orientations that were reassuring, facing the ambiguity in the perilous process of maturation. She was truly an angel of mercy. She has now reclaimed her rightful station in the celestial kingdom where she always belonged.

She incessantly lamented the fact that she had been denied the opportunity of getting an education. She had been compelled to stay home to assist with the household duties. Day in and day out she ruefully bemoaned her lack of "savoir faire" as she labeled it. This was indeed bewildering to me.

So on one occasion I ventured to tell her what was in my heart. "You have no need of what lies beyond what you possess. The treasure that already abides in your heart far exceeds any knowledge you might have accumulated in years of study. It is a gift that radiates from your soul, warming the hearts of those in your midst. It is a gift that is the wonder and envy of those in your entourage, professors, priests, teachers, who have spent most of their lives in the pursuit of knowledge. These men and women know that what you possess cannot be taught or learned. It is a treasure that providence in its beneficence has showered upon you. Therefore do not envy what they have gained through years in endless labor and study. The ethereal treasure so lavishly bestowed upon you is more enviable and transcends all they may have gained so arduously." Although Yvonne was gratified by this sentiment, she was undeniably not convinced.

Germaine was the second daughter. She was born after the family arrived in the west. From my earliest recollections she was the cause of continual disputes, altercations, even quarrels in the household.

My dad could not tolerate her shenanigans. According to him she was the incarnation of provocation. These quarrels even gravitated down to the siblings in the household. My mother defended and protected her jealously from my father's furious tirades. Mercifully so, as should those controversial individuals not be barricaded behind a sheltering angel, they'd drown themselves in the raging turbulence of the tempestuous billows they themselves create (stir). Still, Germaine was not mean. On the contrary, she was generous to a fault. She was just determined to assert herself as a unique individual, come what may! Traditions, conventions, propriety, conformity, were all restraining terms to her, violating freedom or personal liberty. So she openly defied all these acceptable standards. That was, at the time, easily done. It was, then, inappropriate for women to do this or that or the something or other. In fact it was not appropriate for women to do not much of anything at all.

Germaine enjoyed swimming, dancing, and especially, clad in a pair of men's trousers, get on a horse and ride with the wind. She would rush through her work and then she felt free to do as she pleased.

Later these activities she persisted in doing would have been deemed commendable. Therefore the imposition of unreasonable restrictions on personal liberty was the true perpetrator; not the one who treasured her freedom above all else! To the father, who had Victorian moral standards, strict conformity to the acceptable conventional norms was crucial. Thus the daughter's defiant attitude resulted in severe conflict. The disagreement among the siblings centered around and was the consequence of "borrowing". Germaine loved to wear out her clothes, then "borrow" everyone else's, with or without permission. Which is of course a normal occurrence in most households. But when it happens incessantly it can be most unpleasant!

Laurence was a fun loving guy. He delighted in dancing, laughter, joking and playing the clown. Teasing was his forte. He exulted in tormenting, tantalizing until everyone was in tears. He triumphed when there was nothing but screaming, screeching, fighting, everywhere in the house. Utter bedlam! Pandemonium! That was when my oldest sister, who was always left in charge, her nerves completely frazzled, would tear her hair out in desperation.

He made a joke out of everything, even the flu. When he thought the monster was about to attack, he'd fight it tooth and nail. Sitting there with his favorite lunch, a bowl of bread and milk, he'd say, "All you have to do is lunch it out." On one occasion an intermittent worker reappeared on the fourth day after working one day and being absent for two. As he (the worker) had been badly needed, Laurence asked him why he hadn't come. "I bought food with the money you gave me," he said, "then I hunted for food the next two days." "Well," retorted my brother, "that's all well and good but I'd hate like hell to have to chase a rabbit every morning for my breakfast." It is very probable that the repair work was never completed.

This fun loving brother was overjoyed when he joined the household's makeshift concerts. He played the violin with the left hand. Marie-Anne would at times join him in a violin duet. He loved "beauty". Marie-Anne was his favorite sister because she was so beautiful and so gifted. He also had a horse, Pearl, that was his pride and joy. It was such a gorgeous, intelligent horse. It broke my heart when he sold it.

Resourceful and industrious he always managed to find employment. With the proceeds of his meager wages (50 cents a day) he had managed to buy himself a bicycle. It was the envy of the whole household and even of the neighbourhood. As a young and handsome youth he fell passionately in love with a nurse in training with my sister. He would have given his life for her. It broke his heart when the whole affair came to naught.

As a youth, Laurence was unaware that he had an infected appendicitis. While working on a threshing crew, two containers had carelessly been filled, one with gasoline and the other with drinking water. His throat being parched, Laurence grabbed the first container and before he could eject the gas in his mouth, he swallowed a bit of it. Even though it was ever so little it caused the appendicitis to rupture. He was rushed to the hospital. An emergency operation was performed on arrival. However the distance to the hospital was considerable and before he arrived the infection had already spread all over his abdomen. Although the operation was successful the doctor had to insert several tubes into his body to allow the infection to drain. His condition was critical. The doctor feared for his life. When we visited him he was in excruciating pain. He was so thin that his huge blue gray eyes predominated his whole face. In fact those great beautiful eyes seemed the only feature left, he was so drawn and pale. There was such a foul odor permeating the room that it is a wonder that the unfortunate invalid was able to tolerate it.

Laurence was in the hospital for a considerable length of time, but he miraculously recovered. The doctor, in spite of his diligent care, was incredulous. He had nicknamed his patient the "miracle man". He was not the only one concerned about the patient's life. My mother, even though we lived miles from the hospital and had limited funds, visited him regularly.

To attempt or even dare form an accurate portrayal of Laurence as a lad without picturing him with his 22 rifle and his little log shack would be deceptive and unrealistic. They were part of who he was. Of course there were also numerous handmade sleds and slingshots that he delighted in sharing with the rest of us.

But the log shacks and the 22 rifle were the most important. He built these little log shacks all over the farm, or wherever there were trees that had been left standing. They were his and as soon as he had finished constructing one, he'd proudly call all the girls for the unveiling. One of these was spacious and well constructed. It had several windows and was big enough for all to use as a playhouse. The girls decorated it tastefully and artistically - it even had curtains on the windows. Some of these "masterpieces" were small. On one occasion everyone was invited in the smallest creation. Unfortunately when it was time to get out, no one was able to squeeze out the narrow door. Each one in turn had to be pushed and pulled out. This was, to say the least, most demeaning for both the guests and the boyish entrepreneur!

Laurence's skill as a marksman was phenomenal. He kept the family's larder well stocked with wild meat. Grouse, prairie chickens, partridges, wild ducks, even rabbits formed a welcome variety or change from the usual meat supply. At times when the pork and beef was unavailable, the wild meat he hunted was the only source available.

Soon he too was gone. The drama of his life is another story that remains and needs to be told. There are so many more, so many, many more events, spectacular incidences that cannot be justifiably crammed into a few miserly words. The drama of each individual's life would fill volumes. Especially if the narrator only knew or had any inkling of what transpires within the depths of someone's heart. As I write these lines, those incidences come flooding back, overflowing the cherished memories that already cling, treasured in my heart.

Jeannette Romaniuk

It was Hélène that the fairies endowed with wisdom, the most precious of all gifts. With that wisdom came rationality, plain common sense, always knowing what is the proper thing to do in a crisis. Compound that by an impeccable moral code and the culmination is exceptional. But that's not all, as amplification and perhaps a crowning bonus (icing on the cake?), they left her an exquisite artistic talent. On this earth, where we tread, gifts are not evenly distributed. Some possess many, others just enough to get by, while some have none at all. "Ask not," the Holy Bible says, "why". God in His sublime enlightenment chose only those who had the strength and integrity of character to bear such a formidable trust. God must have in his eminent judgment said, "I confide these most precious gifts unto your custody. So, use them wisely, in such a way that their influence will be felt, wherever you may wander."

Indeed these endowments, these gifts, manifesting themselves as special talents, powers, etc. are a sacred trust confided into the hands of a few chosen ones, who are but messengers, emissaries, whose missions are to spread, share, and propagate their prodigious marvels. Those chosen must have the strength, integrity and nobility of character to bear the implications of such a formidable trust. For they may not use its wonders for their own selfish aggrandisement, but for the benefit of others. History is replete with men who have been bequeathed with such extraordinary powers. They have been instrumental in the progress and enjoyment of mankind. For example, Mozart, the prodigious genius, whose creations will be the ecstasy of his fellowman till the end of times. And Einstein, whose scientific theories have rocked the earth. Without geniuses such as these our world would not be the same. They have paved our journey through life with comfort and joy.

Envy such as these! Never! Let us rejoice that fate has permitted someone in our midst, close to us, to have been chosen. That someone in our midst possessed the righteousness and courage to merit such a formidable trust. Envy them! Indeed no! The Almighty has, in His wisdom, chosen the meritorious ones!

For most, the burden would have been too formidable. The endowments possessed would instill such anxiety that like the rich man's steward in the Holy Bible, they would bury them, camouflaged jealously, in the fortress of their own selfishness. Most strive and struggle just to keep their heads above water, holding their breath less they sink. Indeed most drift there, not daring to breathe, less they engender turbulence. The towering waters are dangerously menacing out there. Most, agonizing about the morrow are oblivious of today. Complacent, they are content to let the strong lead the way - hither thither wherever that current may drift, to and fro.

From her earliest years, Hélène's remarkable and talented personality was obvious. It was evident that she possessed a superior intelligence. She was in good health, physically and mentally advanced for her age, which is characteristic of gifted children. One of her most outstanding traits was her determination. She appeared to have laid out her path in life from the moment she was born and to know where that path would lead her. Her tenacity and strength of character was conspicuous even in the cradle. During the Spanish Flu, she had decided that no one but my mother was to rock her cradle. That was of course impossible. My mother, grievously ill, had been unconscious for almost two weeks. My grandmother, the merciful angel, would silently and imperceptively try to rock the cradle. As little as she was, she knew that that hand was not her mother's.

I am not aware of any ostentatious incidences during Hélène's preschool years. Excepting, perhaps, that she, like Cecile, was meticulous. She could not tolerate imperfection, slovenliness, and most of all immorality. She insisted that propriety be maintained in all aspects of human activity and conduct.

What she was especially particular about was her own personal attire. For economic reasons all the family's wearing apparel was home made. To the rest of the family, it was immaterial. They were thankful to have something to wear. But Hélène, being a perfectionist, could not tolerate clothes that did not fit properly to her taste. She considered the fact that she was forced to wear and adapt to clothes that were unsuitable and uncomfortable insufferable. She must undoubtedly have been most grateful when she could design and sew her own clothes.

It was at our little country school that Hélène first distinguished herself as a brilliant and gifted student. It was there that her superior intelligence was fully realized, both by her teachers and her parents. She amazed her teachers. The mastery of new concepts, in any field of study, presented no problem to her.

At times gifted students present a challenge for a teacher, especially in classrooms where all levels of ability are represented. This situation exists in rural areas. Children come from homes where parents have various levels of education. Sometimes none at all. These children cannot compete with those of average abilities, let alone with those that have superior intelligence. That was the situation confronting the rural teacher in that small community. The gifted students like Hélène (are) were far more advanced. The frustrated teacher was often at a loss to provide these students with sufficient activities to occupy them while they waited for the less capable to "catch up". That must have been what occurred one day in that little rural school. The teacher must have been debating and contemplating an activity for Hélène, who had finished her assignment in a flash. Subsequently he told her to memorize a portion of the poem, "The Charge of the Light Brigade," a poem the class had recently studied. Evidently he intended to keep her busy until the other students had finished the previous assignment and the class could proceed to a new task. To the teacher's astonishment she, long before the others had finished their work, came up to his desk and declared, "I know it." "How many stanzas did you memorize?" inquired the teacher. "I know it all," she insisted. "But you barely had time to sit down," retorted the startled teacher, in disbelief. "I will recite it for you if you wish," continued Hélène. And so she proceeded to recite the whole poem to the incredulous teacher. It was rumored that she memorized the whole text, which is at least three pages in length, in five minutes. Although that may have been an exaggeration, the achievement was still no less extraordinary.

Shell River School No. 3090

The school was an English Immersion School. During regular class time, all subjects were taught in English, with the exception of the last hour. In that hour French Literature, grammar, and religion were taught. Fortunately most of the district residents were of French descent, and the students therefore were able to grasp and retain this conglomeration of knowledge all presented in their native tongue. One student (only one) was English, however. It was impossible for him to cram all this information presented in a foreign language. He never learned to speak the language or master the concepts involved in that one hour of instruction.

At the time, in the province of Saskatchewan, it was compulsory to write departmental examinations at the end of each year, from the eighth to the twelfth year. These examinations were prepared and corrected by the department of education and included all basic subjects. In grade eight Hélène wrote these examinations. She obtained the highest standing in French of all Saskatchewan students. She was awarded a gold medal and some historical documents written in French (the story of the gold medal is a legend in itself).

In rural areas students were expected, after their eighth grade, to finish their education by following courses offered by the department of education. The books were supplied to a certain level and for a reasonable fee the assignments were corrected. This was of course what Hélène and I, following right behind at her heels, did. The assignments were never corrected, as the family could not afford the fee. She, endowed with such superior ability, along with the freedom to proceed at her own rate, voraciously devoured with a passion all this amazing new knowledge. In spite of the obstacles constantly in her way, she never wavered. And obstacles there were! Not one but trillions of them. It is impossible to recall at what level the books were not provided with the courses. This was a major obstacle. Providence intervened. The neighbors (they were providence, no less!) youngest son, who was a year ahead of Hélène, lent or gave her the books. These were passed on to me afterwards. The second seemingly insurmountable impediment was the interminable chores that were crucial to the family's survival. Hélène, being physically strong, felt obligated and assumed voluntarily the most strenuous of these tasks. Subsequently she worked continuously during the day, unable to devote any time to her studies. In the evening and late at night she managed to cram all this knowledge until she completed her grade eleven. It is incredulous, absolutely incomprehensible how she managed to have the strength to work all day and study all night. At times she was still studying at three o'clock in the morning. (My book was on the floor and I was sleeping on my feet by that time). But she was undaunted.

When my mother became extremely ill she decided to become a nurse. She claimed that the frustration of being helpless not having the knowledge or the expertise to alleviate my mother's suffering was instrumental to her decision. She trained at the Holy Family Hospital in Prince Albert. The nursing school offered both the academic theoretical expertise and the practical training synonymously. She excelled in both.

During her training, Hélène's remuneration was a scant five dollars a month. Yet she managed to send gifts to everyone in the family at Christmas time. She also managed to buy a radio. This radio was a tremendous asset to the younger members of the family. Although most could understand, speak and read the English language they lacked the ability to pronounce it correctly. The radio was instrumental in contributing an accurate model to follow. Later, when she became a registered nurse and acquired a nursing position, she regularly sent money to help support the family.

Although Hélène was strong physically, and her strength may have been instrumental in saving her life, there were two critical episodes in which she survived fatal illnesses. The first occurred during the Spanish Flu. Born in 1917, she was but an infant when the curse of that deadly disease was at the height of its most malignant and devastating ravages. She was considered terminally ill. The parish priests, on their rounds of mercy visiting the sick, thought it would be a miracle if she survived. So did my grandparents! One miserable day, at a most critical point in the child's illness, the family feared that she would not live through the night. The symptoms were getting increasingly more severe. The fever was dangerously high and mounting continually. She would have hysterical seizures during the pyretic attacks and fall into a state of convulsion. That evening a stranger appeared at the door. As soon as he entered the house, the man sensed that something was dreadfully wrong. He realized that the whole household (at least those who were well) was overwhelmed with anxiety and hopelessness concerning the grave condition of the child. He looked at the patient and made an utterly astounding statement, "There is only one way to save this child," he declared. "You must put a few drops of turpentine in a spoonful of sugar and make sure she swallows it." "Oh, but that would most positively poison her," protested the grandmother. "Well," rejoined the stranger, "as you are well aware she will surely die without any intervention." As a last resort the desperate grandmother reluctantly administered the hazardous medication. It is uncertain if the dosage was repeated. Low and behold the child immediately began to recover. Soon she was well and flourishing. The controversial medication, or a miracle? Modern doctors would shake their heads in disbelief at such procedures. But it may well be that their prescribed drugs are far more lethal!!

The second time Hélène miraculously survived a critical illness was when the persisting recurrence of appendicitis in the household had almost reached an epidemic level. Practically all the older members of the family had this appendage removed surgically because it was infected. What engendered this dreadful affliction was unknown at the time. Both Hélène and Laurence barely escaped with their lives. It may be that Hélène had suffered in silence for a considerable length of time.

She was not known to complain, ever! When the appendix ruptured she was rushed to the hospital. The infection had spread dangerously. As a consequence of the delay, the period of convalescence was greatly extended and painful. The physician had prescribed that Hélène take advantage of the sun's healing power during these most difficult days of recuperation. It was incredibly disturbing to see how she painfully dragged herself into the sunlight and back in again, longing for her ailing body to be restored to health. Yet she bore the trauma of all this miserable discomfort and distress in silence.

Sleeping Beauty's beneficent fairies must surely have visited our humble domain as they alone could have cast such magical, bewitching charms upon some of the members of our household. They endowed one with wisdom, Hélène, and sound judgment (prudence), one with virtue, Yvonne, and another with beauty.

Marie Anne,Laurence Gaumond.

Beauty was bestowed upon Marie-Anne. And in their lavish generosity, the fairies crowned this gift with musical talent, an enchanting melodious voice, and a captivating personality as a bonus. She possessed big brown eyes, an oval shaped face framed by golden brown hair. Her captivating poise and irresistible charisma culminated the splendor of her charm. She was sought by all, young or old, but especially by the youth of the surrounding vicinity, or any young man who had even once laid eyes upon her.

She played the violin by note or by ear (or any other instrument for that matter). She too had inherited my mother's phenomenal musical talent. She played the violin during our makeshift charivari concerts; she played for dances, but most of the time she played for pure enjoyment. Besides, she sang like an angel. It was nonetheless a Herculean task to persuade her to sing in public. It is very probable that she preferred to be as inconspicuous as possible as she was a very private person. Her popularity as a dancing partner was exceptional. Light as a feather and skillful she was as gracious on the dance floor as she was beautiful in appearance. She won dancing contests on many occasions, dancing the French Minuet.

Her alluring beauty, her glamour complemented by her extraordinary musical talent would undeniably have made her a star, had she had the opportunity. Armed with these prodigious, sensational characteristics she would have become a celebrity, the rave of Hollywood.

From the very beginning Marie-Anne's life was beset with critical predicaments; near disasters! As an infant she fell down a huge flight of stairs (nearly six feet) landing face down below. She must have been rather seriously hurt because she cried for a long time. The accident caused a great deal of anxiety and torment. Everyone feared that the injury might cause permanent damage to her brain. Everyone was filled with anguish and compassion, commiserating with the child's suffering. She apparently recovered without any ill effects.

Not long after that tragic accident, Marie-Anne became seriously ill. She may have been eighteen months or perhaps two years old at the time. It was a strange illness. As doctors were non-existent, my parents did the best they could to care for her. The whole family was at a loss nonetheless as the symptoms were remarkably uncommon and bizarre. The child would throw herself as far as she could and scream with pain. She had hysterical seizures and no one could hold her. My mother thought it resembled St. Vitres dance, however no one was able to diagnose the ailment with certainty. The strangest part of this incidence was that my dad thought the child was throwing a temper tantrum. He was furious. Everyone was completely horrified at his reaction. It is unclear what his intentions were but that he was angry there was no doubt. I'll never forget how terrified I was by the father's anger and the child's anguish. Although only about four, the scene will, as it flashes back distinctly before my eyes, follow me the rest of my days.

Nonetheless, Marie-Anne seemed to be the only one to possess the gifts that captured my father's heart. In the evening, after work, while smoking his pipe she'd be sitting on his lap for hours. He was decidedly more lenient with her than with the rest of us. For instance, she was never coerced to assist in the endless housekeeping and farming chores. Perhaps it was her placid and tranquil nature that won my dad's favor. Or was it, as some of the family claims, that she was his favorite, plain and simple! The only occasion upon which he raved and roared at her was when he caught her and the two younger sisters at the very top of the towering trees in the pasture. Which is not surprising!!

Her quiet, unobtrusive nature was complemented by a sharp and cunning wit. She'd be in a pensive and meditating mien, yet all at once she'd utter such an amazing and humorous observation that everyone laughed. One day as she was intently watching her brother hungrily bolt down his supper, she remarked, "Eat, George, eat! You'll never eat any younger." One of the most remarkable characteristics in Marie-Anne's personality was her love for cats. She was always surrounded by cats...cats...cats...dozens of them. She cuddled them, petted them, and held two or three in her arms at once. She treated them like children, her babies. Her love of cats was so extraordinary that she was nicknamed "la mere au chat", the mother cat.

The attribute that surpassed all others was her calm, composed dignity. There was more enticing magnetism in that serene, tranquil composer (poise) than a thousand words could have achieved.

And that was what made her so popular! She was the dream of every young man in the county. In spite of all her gifts, her popularity, her beauty, fate did not look down on her with favor. Her marriage at sixteen was a disaster! She was left with three children to support and nurture. She never faltered, nonetheless. Even though her health was poor, she managed to get a "nurse's aide" certificate. Her courage and valiant nature proved equal to her gifted personality. She too has joined the throng of angels that inhabit the celestial kingdom. May she enrapture the heavens with the charm of her melodious voice!

Juliette was a unique and distinct individual in every sense of the word. She had all these sui generis, nonpariel characteristics that had a sophistication all their own. For instance, it was practically impossible to get her to go to bed (come what may) at night. A veritable night hawk! She wanted to talk, to do things, or perhaps just to make sure that she didn't miss anything. That, to my dad, was intolerable; He felt that evenings were his time to relax, to smoke his pipe in peace, without the pandemonium, the hullabaloo of the crowded and stressful turmoil of the day. He insisted on being left undisturbed in that period. He was most perturbed when anyone trespassed on his space, his time. And that is exactly what Juliette did when she stayed up till the wee hours of the morning. He was exasperated, "I can't even have that little bit of time to myself to relax," he lamented. Another one of her antics was that she insisted on drinking vinegar. She seemed to have an insatiable craving for it. The rest of us had to guard the pickle jar with our lives, otherwise she would have drunk the whole vinegar juice after the pickles were gone. Sometimes she'd slice some raw onions in vinegar and relish that. She just loved any food that was sour, like raw rhubarb dipped in salt. It was feared that so much vinegar could be injurious to her health.

When she was very young Juliette was afflicted by a strange disease. Both her legs were paralyzed. For the longest time she was unable to walk and had to be carried everywhere. It's a wonder that no one suspected that it may have been polio.

Juliette was my oldest sister's godchild. It was, apparently, the reason why she was hers and my mother's favorite. These two showered her with affection and privileges. They were much more indulgent with her than with any of the other brothers and sisters. She could do no wrong in their eyes. In any skirmish or disagreement the blame was always imposed upon the other, whoever that may have been. Of course she took advantage of this. What child wouldn't. This sometimes caused resentment and pain among those who were the scapegoat and were punished guilty or not in all circumstances.

Be that as it may, Juliette turned out to be the most unselfish, magnanimous individual known. Her ability to think of herself last, to deny herself until the needs of everyone else had been met must have been inherited from my mother. That generous lady never had a bite of food until everyone else had been satiated. And if her self-sacrificing and generous nature did not parallel that of her older sister, it most certainly ran a close second. For both were the embodiment of benevolence and generosity.

There is yet another trait of Juliette's character that should not be ignored or forgotten. As a child she too was a tomboy, joining Marie-Anne and Cecile in their daring exploits. Climbing trees, crawling in Laurence's tiny log shacks that stood all over the farm, swimming in sloughs. Subsequent to those audacious group escapades one could readily fall in the trap of classifying the three as one. Or to lean towards the tendency to stereotype the trio with the same personal characteristics. Hence neglecting the emphasis on each individual's traits.

The three wore dresses that had been sewn from dyed sugar sacks. This material was very stiff, similar to canvas. The three girls would get these dresses so dirty, doing all their shenanigans that it was almost impossible to get them clean. A floor brush had to be used to scrub these dresses to some semblance of cleanliness. The girls found it most demeaning that their dresses were scrubbed with the same brush as the floor. It was indeed regrettable that these adventurous girls were not clad in more suitable garments such as denim slacks. Perhaps those were not in style or perhaps it was inappropriate for girls to wear them. It is much more probable that denim overalls were non-existent at that time.

It is strange that, regardless of their relationship, some folks seem to be part of one's whole life. While with others, it feels as if you were on a blind date when reminiscing about their lives. The secret longings and aspirations of their spirits have somewhat become illusive. The lives of these dear ones are mysteriously unknown. How true that one doesn't realize and appreciate the value of a treasure until it has, like sand, slipped through the fingers. How lamentable that it should be so! If it were only possible, remotely feasible, to retrace those erring steps, go back and redress what was so thoughtlessly, heedlessly, insensitively neglected along the way. Then with loving hands these precious jewels (bits) would be locked away into the most cherished recesses of the heart.

Cécile was the youngest of the girls. She was one of the trio, "the three Musketeers", as they were nicknamed. Together, these adventurous lasses constantly delighted in lively, playful exploits. One episode after another, their shenanigans were endless. Happily and surprisingly they were not bound by the endless toils of farm life. The three of them reveled in the beauty, the freedom of the wide-open spaces. Swimming, climbing trees and mountains, walking, berry picking and more, filled their delightful childhood days.

Looking back, it appears that the youngest of the trio was in very poor health. In the morning she was absolutely miserable, evidently she was ill, until she had had her breakfast. It was imperative that she had some form of nourishment immediately after she got out of bed. Whatever tasks were in the process had to be laid aside, and breakfast prepared for her. Mother irrevocably insisted upon it. At the time it appeared unreasonable. Sometimes my sister was in the process of kneading the bread, the dough sticking to her hands, but she had to stop, wash her hands and prepare breakfast. There was no alternative! Being young and lacking the understanding, those responsible for this task were most disgruntled. It seemed, then, so unfair!!! Looking back, it is apparent that this child, like my dad, had low blood sugar. It is urgent that those who suffer from this condition be provided with nourishment instantly when needed. Mother must have known that the consequences of any delay can be serious.

First Communion Day! That was indeed a spectacular, memorable day. A day that undoubtedly will never be forgotten. In fact it was a day that no one in the family will ever forget. At the time all the children in the parish made their first communion together in a group. It was an awe-inspiring celebration. The girls wore white dresses and a veil, much like a bride. The boys wore a black or blue suit with a white ribbon tied on their forearm. They marched in pairs, the girls in one line and the boys in the other as they approached the altar. The first communicants were the manifestation of angels recently descended from their celestial kingdom to the passing (empty) realism of the earth. The atmosphere breathed an ambience of mystery and of the supernatural!

At that time it was compulsory to fast before receiving Holy Communion. It was obligatory to abstain from both food and water from the previous midnight.

On that fateful day the whole family was already in the vehicle ready to depart for the celebration. That is everyone but Cécile and Juliette! Cécile was proudly attired in her beautiful communion dress and veil, looking radiantly lovely. Just before she climbed into the vehicle followed by Juliette she shrieked, "I drank!" Of course, that was the end of the communion celebration for the family that day. No one breathed a word! Everyone was speechless, overwhelmed with empathy and sympathy for the devastation, the utter dejection, the poor child was experiencing.

Many memories of childhood are resuscitated as I write these lines. For instance, the extreme cold of winter and intense summer heat was unbearable for Cécile. Whereas the rest of us just accepted the weather as a sine qua non, she seemed unable to tolerate or endure its ramifications. That also may have been the consequence of her frail physical nature.

Cécile was meticulous in all aspects of her nature. Excellence was the only standard that she would accept or permit. Perfection had to be attained in all of daily living. Personal health habits, manner of dress, sanitation were attended with precise care. But it was in her housekeeping that this characteristic most evidently manifested itself. Every detailed chore was done with microscopic care. Wherever she was the whole place sparkled. It was as if she sterilized everything daily.

Her moral standards were as stringent as her other expectations. The demands that she imposed upon herself were not humanly attainable. At least not by an ordinary mortal with all its human imperfections and frailties. Again, excellence was the only criteria acceptable in her book. Excesses of any kind, even gourmandizing, were considered deserving of hell fire. Where.... where does that leave the rest of us? Maybe her motto was "many are called but few are chosen," from the bible.

She had set her standards so high that she thought the only place or profession in which she could achieve such excellence was by withdrawing from the world. So she entered the convent and became a "nun" in the service of the Lord. As a novitiate she professed and practiced her faith and beliefs with intense fervor. The depth and intensity of her dedication concerned the Mother Superior who feared for Cécile's health. Therefore Mother Superior advised her to go out into the world and meditate profoundly. This would enable her to know if she had chosen wisely, to contemplate and reflect profoundly before making the crucial decision that she was meant to be a nun and live in seclusion, away from the world. It was the Reverend Mother's sincere opinion that she had made the wrong decision. She was too serious. The extreme precision in which she performed her residential duties and extraordinary devotion in which she pursued her religious professions might be injurious to her health. Her frail nature would never withstand or endure the rigorous demands community life imposes. Subsequently, Cécile went back to live with my parents. It was apparently a very difficult period in her life. She had many internal problems to solve. She eventually married and had three wonderful sons. It is unknown if in her heart she found peace and contentment while she lived in the convent.

Noel Gaumond, & son Raymond.

Raymond was unique in a special way. It is true that every person in the household was unique and different from everyone else. But Raymond had a uniqueness all his own. To begin with, he was the only one in the family born in the hospital, and then he had a severe case of jaundice. This was followed by an extreme case of eczema, or the seven-year itch, as the local people called it. There was no "Lanacane" at the time, no medicine at all to ease the insupportable itch emanating from this disease. The sole respite from the anguish was bathing in a solution of soda and water. The relief was not very effective and long lasting. It was an absolute merry-go-round. First the washtub was filled with lukewarm water in which baking soda had been added. Then the child sat in the tub until the distress of the sting was appeased. Then we'd take him out and sponge dry him. In approximately thirty minutes it all started again. The unbearable itch, the frenzied agitation, the frantic dancing and screaming, and the bathing. This went on and on. As soon as the child's torment came back to oppress him his exasperation would drive him into a frenzy. Then naturally the unfortunate child would become hysterical. My father thought that our efforts to alleviate the child's torment were negligent, that we were irresponsible, and that we lacked compassion for our brother. Both my sister and I were severely reprimanded.

Raymond had other problems with his health. He eventually overcame all these problems and became a strong, healthy lad. Nonetheless, during the years that he was afflicted with so many illnesses, the family treated him with great consideration and solitude. He was allowed to do much as he pleased, more or less. He became thoroughly spoiled (I was the official babysitter at the time). He insisted on being carried everywhere. Toilet training became an almost insurmountable task.

Soon all these problems were forgotten. Raymond's remarkable personality compensated for all the troubles he had been through. He had inherited his mother's wisdom, her musical talents, her beautiful singing voice, and most important of all, her steadfast moral integrity.

It was pure ecstasy to hear his melodious, high pitch imitation of my mother's songs. He knew the lyrics' every word and could sing their every melody. He could play almost any musical instrument, but the accordion was the instrument he preferred. The young adored his music and exhorted him to play incessantly.

He was also a voracious reader. Wherever he lived he was surrounded with books. Comic books and science fiction were his favorite subjects. He loved any material dealing with scientific research and projected scientific discoveries, inventions, and explorations.

This interest and pursuit of scientific knowledge served him well. He claimed that before he had read about the theory behind the splitting of the atom, he had calculated and figured out the process. On another occasion he performed myriad experiments to determine and discover an inexhaustible source of natural energy. I am not at liberty to divulge the source or the elements he used in his experiments, as it was confidential. He claimed that he could never forgive himself if his inventions and discoveries fell in the wrong hands, or if they were used as a tool to financially oppress the poor. But this again exceeds the limits of this tale and must be told at length to be fully appreciated.

However, excluding Raymond's unfaltering moral integrity would be a serious misrepresentation of the most outstanding attribute abiding in his personality. His staunch moral standards were never compromised. It was the essence of who he truly was. He could not tolerate the lack of self-control and self-discipline in any form. He firmly believed that a human being has been endowed with intelligence and therefore should use that wisdom to guide his choices and behavior in a rational manner. He abhorred alcohol and cigarette smoke and would leave when anyone dared to smoke or drink in his presence. This characteristic was so conspicuous even when Raymond was yet a very young child that it astonished and amazed many adults.

His name was Gerard, my little brother. He is now one of God's cherubs and dwells with the angels in the celestial kingdom on the other side of the firmament. Even during his fleeting, momentary sojourn on this earth, for he was not yet two when he died, he must have been ethereal. He was so phenomenal, so adorable, yellow-haired, blue-eyed, he was an exact replica of all the divine spiritual beings that awaited him.

It was so painful to let him go - he was so loved, so treasured!

St. Joseph must have, from his heavenly home, wanted Gerard to follow in his footsteps, for the child was from morning till night, with a hammer in his hand, constantly pounding nails in the cover of the bread box. Was it St. Joseph who claimed the Cherubim carpenter to assist him in some celestial fabrication?

The child was obsessed with the outdoors. He persistently managed, oblivious to anyone, to steal or sneak out of doors and wander around the yard. He enjoyed watching the birds, the farm animals and the fresh air.

That habit caused a great deal of anguish to everyone in the family. It was my duty to care for both Gerard and Raymond who was the youngest. In the early morning Gerard constantly managed to sneak out before he was properly dressed. As soon as he was spotted wandering around the yard in his nightshirt he would be brought to the house and dressed. Many times, in chilly temperature, I would find him scantily dressed, barefooted, and chilled to the bone and rush him inside to get him warm and dressed. That memory still tears my heart apart. When it was my dad who found the child, it caused a veritable uproar. He raved and ranted, "How can anyone be that irresponsible?" he roared. Yet in spite of the guilt and wretched feelings in my heart, and the severe reprimands from my father, the incidence kept repeating itself incessantly.

Subsequently Gerard contacted pneumonia. He was given every care that is feasible in a home. His condition was too serious and it progressively deteriorated. In desperation, my mother tried to locate the local doctor and persuade him to either make a house call or prescribe medication. Alas the doctor could not be found as he had been summoned on another urgent call. It was too late. Till the very last, the child insisted that I be the only one to hold him and not leave him. I still feel the anguish, the pain of his bereavement. The feeling of guilt, like a dagger still pierces my heart.

Everlastingly too late we torture ourselves, wondering why, oh why, did we not do what was crucial until it was too late and all was lost.

Many cousins living in the district were so dear to our family that it is hard not to include them as our very own. There was one in particular, Maurice. This cousin had apparently made the grandparents' home his permanent residence. It was permanent that is until he came up with some shenanigan that almost drove my uncle out of his mind. Which happened on several occasions!

Maurice was an absolute scientific genius. Even though he had little formal education, his knowledge and understanding of scientific principles was phenomenal. It appeared to be a natural talent or perhaps it emanated from his exceptionally inquisitive mind. "I must find out how it works," was his dictum. And that is precisely what he proceeded to do. One of these investigations occurred when he was ten years old, living at my grandparents' place. My uncle had just purchased a brand new tractor. He was especially proud. Very few farmers could afford such luxury and most still used horses. It happened while my uncle was away on business. Using that opportunity, Maurice proceeded to take the whole machine apart, bit-by-bit, engine and all! He had to see how it worked, so he said! And it was at this point when all the parts of the machine were strewn about that the uncle came home. Undeniably this man went insane with rage and desperation. There was no doubt in his mind that the tractor was now a pile of rubbish. In despair he thought of the enormous sum he had spent for this machine only to be forced to continue using horses to cultivate the land. Trembling with fear, my cousin hardly dared say a word. However he gathered up his courage and said, "I can put it together again, I know how!" Without a word, my uncle turned and walked away.

Sometime later, grandfather happened to glance through the window. To his utter amazement he saw the tractor all in one piece as good as ever. "Son, did you not say that your tractor was ruined and that the parts were strewn all over the yard," he asked. "Yes," replied the uncle, "and so it was." "Well" said the father, "there isn't a thing wrong with that machine now. Or so it seems to me." Subsequently the astounded uncle inspected the machine meticulously tooth and nail. It was exactly and precisely reassembled. Not a bolt or a part out of place. "I told you that I could put it together again," declared the culprit. All those who witnessed this amazing feat were speechless. It was incredible! This young lad who wasn't yet ten years had succeeded in an accomplishment that few adults could perform.

Years later he continued on his quest of discovery. He could not rest until he had found the "how" and "why" of his environment. He was often lost in thought twirling a strand of hair on his forehead, until he had resolved a problem. Then he had to explain the whole process to someone. It was a compulsion. He'd give detailed explanations to anyone who'd listen - going on and on. Most people were annoyed because he never stopped talking. Most avoided him like the plague because they didn't have a clue what he was talking about. They did not realize that they, and not Maurice, were to blame. The extent of their scientific knowledge was too restricted to allow them to understand what Maurice was saying. He was thinking at a level at which most could never hope to attain. He was alone on a plane few could reach, isolated by the wisdom he so lavishly possessed. Looking back, I feel the pain of his loneliness and understand his frustration, but the scope of his world is too far-flung, too vast for me to comprehend and share even now! Alas, it is too late to tell him so. Too late!

There was another incident in that man's life that was so bizarre, so unusual, that it certainly couldn't repeat itself. Not in a million years! It happened while the men were working in the bush in Big River County. For some reason or other Maurice always seemed to be with the men in the family. And so was Uncle Charles. Perhaps they were partners in the fulfillment of certain contracts. Well, when he was yet quite young, Maurice managed to acquire a gun, his first gun. He was thrilled! Besides his enthusiasm bubbling over with excitement about the gun, he couldn't wait to go hunting. My dad, being a cautious man, was quite apprehensive. He knew Maurice was extremely impulsive and extremely quick to react. He warned the "would be" hunter about the fact that guns were not toys and that he should use it with extreme security precautions. These warnings were of course disregarded. My dad was exasperated. Later when he related the incidence to my mother he was in a panic. "Maurice turned a deaf ear to what I was saying," he complained, using his arm as the barrel of the gun he reenacted the whole scene. "First thing I knew Maurice was shooting at anything that moved. All I could hear was 'pow, pow, pow', a pause, and 'pow, pow, pow' on and on. Again I warned Maurice to make sure he knew what he was aiming at. But it was no use. He continued this reckless shooting. Even the stepfather thought I was over-reacting. There was no one in the woods so he claimed he couldn't hurt anyone." But he was wrong. There was an old lumberman who had spent his life in the forest. He was a hermit. He did some work in the lumber industry, trapped and hunted for his living. The men knew him well. He seemed to be part of the woods for he was always there. One morning, Maurice took his gun and went hunting. Again he was told to be careful. As usual he kept shooting recklessly, completely overwhelmed by this amazing new wonder. Then tragedy struck. There was a piercing shriek of pain and terror. Maurice froze, paralyzed with fear. The second scream left no doubt in his mind. He had shot a man!! In a daze he ran in the direction from which he had heard the scream. And there, bleeding profusely was this huge two hundred pound man, wounded, and lying in the snow. The horror, the shock of this realization brought a rush of energy to our hunter. He flung the gigantic man over his shoulder and carried him to the nearest hospital, Big River, a distance of sixty miles. This miraculous feat is one of life's mysteries. For not only was Maurice an average sized man, weighing approximately 160 pounds, but he maintained that the wounded man's bulk seemed inexplicably light. Perhaps the fear for the man's life rendered him physically senseless and made him incapable of feeling pain, fatigue or emotional torment.

Fortunately the man survived. The wound was not life threatening. It is likely that the injured man could have walked part of the way. In spite of his injury he was a strong man. He didn't have to, as Maurice's momentum, his energy sufficed for both of them. Later Maurice admitted that he had never been so frightened in his whole life. Needless to say he never used a gun irresponsibly in the future. Or it may be that he never hunted again!

So many in such confined, crowded spaces is bound to cause many serious problems. Especially when the number of residents is doubled by permanent non-paying lodgers. Compound that with severe financial difficulties and the situations become insurmountable, an absolute crisis!!

Granted some of the times were extremely difficult, there were other times - times filled with joy and sheer rapture - other times simply ludicrously humorous.

There were so many joyous occasions. They compensated and obliterated the periods of stress and sadness. There were the jubilant amateur concerts when everyone joined in. There were the story times gatherings. Evenings when blood curdling, horrendous tales, sending chills up and down your spine, were alternated with tales that were so preposterous, so hilarious, you were hysterically convulsed with laughter. There were the freakish, unprecedented events. Events that were so absurd and bizarre that the recollection never ceased to be the source of everlasting hilarity for all. Then there were the times when someone did something utterly nonsensical, irrational and became the butt of ceaseless teasing and ridicule. At times the whole family poked fun at an object. For instance, the medicine bag, and the whole scenario that surrounded it. For one thing, that bag posed a veritable threat! No one was exempt from its assault as it descended upon the least unsuspecting head. No one, except perhaps my mother, was cognizant of its medicinal contents. Mac Beth's witches would have had a regular field day brewing its prophetical entrails. Laurence never ceased tormenting my mother about the professed magic of that medicine bag. Nonetheless, my mother truly believed in the valuable medical properties of natural herbs. There was always a pot of herb tea brewing on the back of the stove to ensure the family's good health, and to repel the assaults of any incoming germs.

There were so many ridiculous episodes transpiring in the household that it would take a lifetime to record each and every one of them. Some of these are so ludicrous and so utterly comical that they are priceless. At times we had to refrain from laughing when the event occurred, although we were bursting to do so as someone dear was the target of the joke. However when it was all over, everyone was hysterical with laughter, including the scapegoat.

Many of these events took place during the prohibition. That government decree did not accomplish its projected goal. It did restrict the availability of alcohol at least commercially. Nonetheless, the people retaliated by making their own supply. This was illegal, but when people really want something, they find a way to get it. Most made just enough for their own use. Some took advantage of the alcoholics and brewed enough liquor to supply their regrettable habit (at a price). Many of these bootleggers, as they were called, made a substantial amount of money. One farmer bought a tractor with the proceeds of the sales. It was a local farce. His customers bandying jokingly about the fact that each had bought and paid for a part of that tractor. "I paid for that back wheel," one would say, "it belongs to me." "I paid for the engine," the next client would continue, it's mine! I own more of that machine than you do. An engine is bigger than a wheel."

That banter would go on and on jokingly. Although it was expressed in fun, it was the truth. It would not have been denied even by the proprietor. Everyone in the district knew what this man was doing. It is inconceivable that he wasn't caught.

Most farmers did not produce liquor to make money. Most produced just enough for themselves and as refreshments for their guests. It was for that purpose that my dad did very rarely attempt to produce his own. "Homebrew" the local people nicknamed it. The whole procedure was done secretly during the night behind closed doors or in the basements. All perpetrators were afraid of being reported.

It was a complicated process. First was the fermentation process in which the stock was left undisturbed for a considerable length of time. When the fermentation process was over, the stock was processed in a complicated machine called a distiller. I still have a clear mental picture of this monstrous machine on the stove and tubes everywhere. It seemed to fill the whole house. Scientist (and common sense) interpretation is that it functions on the process of evaporation and condensation. Only the pure alcohol condenses and is captured in containers, the rest evaporates. I still see my dad with his friend operating this complicated procedure. They must have had to wait while the whole affair went through. They sat there, as jovial as can be, telling one tall tale after another. It was a contest to determine who could tell the most outlandish, out and out tale. If my memory does not fail it was Mr. Roger Beautemps who won hands down. That man was an absolute master at spinning a yarn. Yarns that were unrealistic, improbable, far out! But the "fibs" were his masterpiece. His expertise and cunning at concocting these "fibs" was unparalleled.

This distillation bash lasted the whole night through. At dawn the quantity of alcohol collected seemed inconsequential. What did matter was that the whole household was ill from laughing hysterically at those yarns spun throughout the night. Besides his talent, being a master storyteller, this certain Mr. Beautemps had a knack, a special charm about him. He was always able to make my dad laugh heartily and relax. It was so gratifying to see my dad enjoy himself. Of course in the event that any monumental venture such as making homebrew was in the offing this special friend always participated.

Besides the homebrew bashes, there were other phenomenal encounters with the spirits. Wine making episodes! The whole neighbourhood made wine and our family was no exception. Wild fruit abounded in the vicinity - saskatoons, pin cherries, cherries, cranberries. These (and dandelions) make excellent wines. Perhaps there were many batches of wine, produced in the early years, but there are only two that stand out in my memory. At our house the wine was always processed and fermented in large wooden barrels. At a certain time when it was "ready" it was bottled. Everyone in the family joined in this activity. It was fun!

On one occasion, the barrel of wine stood beside the house, ready to be "bottled". That particular batch never did get "bottled"!!! It happened early in the morning, just before dawn, the morning on which the wine was supposed to be "bottled". Pandemonium! A formidable racket! Shouting, pots and pans rattling, things falling, running, the whole house shaking! Everyone jumped out of bed, half naked, and ran downstairs to see what was happening. Perhaps the house was on fire! The only logical conclusion!!! But it was worst than that. There was my mother, dressed in a very short white t-shirt nightie, beside herself with rage. Her fury was so violent that everyone stood there appalled. She was screaming, raving about something we were unaware of. The sight would have been hilarious had it not been so dramatic. For in her hand was a dipper. With this long handled dipper she was flinging the wine as far as she could throw it. How she managed to get that full barrel of wine almost to the edge of the property line is beyond me. She emptied the whole barrel, cursing at the top of her voice, until there wasn't a drop of wine left. She never told us what had provoked such a violent outburst of temper and precipitated such a tempestuous rage, so unlike her. But we guessed.

That scene keeps flashing back before my eyes, crystal clear. My mother, in a mini white t-shirt, fiercely pitching that cursed wine across the road with such momentum that it alighted on and doused the field next to us (section #19).

The second wine episode was not as shockingly chaotic or as emotionally imbued as the first (this statement is debatable as the repercussions could have been catastrophic!). During the fermentation period the wine in the wood barrel, its usual recipient, was left undisturbed. On that particular occasion it may be that the cover was not securely fastened. Nonetheless, when the cover was removed and the wine ready to be processed, low and behold, at the bottom of the barrel, dead as a doornail, was a drowned cat! Another wine calamity! Needless to say no less than the previous batch it was never "bottled". Someone recently very aptly commented "I hope they didn't drink the wine before they found the cat." Mercifully not!!!

These alcoholic brewing ventures unearthed many disturbing thoughts. It is utterly incredulous that my mother even considered allowing alcoholic beverages in her house, let alone brew it. She loathed (absolutely despised) alcohol with a passion. Her vehement hatred for any beverages containing even a drop of the substance was phenomenal, almost bizarre! It was deeply, tenaciously embedded in her soul.

What had been the source from which all this animosity had originated? One can only speculate.

The saber that had inflicted such a painful wound must have been malignantly trenchant indeed!

One day just as my sister Hélène was leaving for school, she reached for her sweater that happened to be on top of the "armoire" next to the medicine bag. How that sweater got there was one of those mysteries that occurred periodically and steadily at the house. As soon as she had put on the sweater she began to jump and dance, pulling hysterically at her sleeve. Everyone watched in amazement. No one was overly alarmed however; as she was such a meticulous person and was especially particular about the clothes she wore. But there was cause for alarm! As we stood watching in astonishment a mouse scrambled out of her sleeve and clambered back to the top of the "armoire". And there in a flash the sweater was violently flung, or more accurately pitched! Hélène must have gone to school without a sweater that day.

How that mouse had escaped the cats is another mystery. We had a whole army of cats. They were in the barn, in the granaries, in the blacksmith's shop, the machine shed, and the house. They were everywhere. And woe to anyone who even dared to abuse these cats either verbally or physically. There was a "built in" animal guardian in the establishment, Marie-Anne. She had been nicknamed "La Mere au Chats" or the "Mother Cat". She just loved these animals! Wherever she was, there was bound to be a dozen or so of these animals in the vicinity.

Our farm was the last on the edge of a vast area of uncultivated land. It included many sections. It was a spacious, immense expanse, where the beauty of nature had been undisturbed. It was an absolute wonderland, a child's paradise! The low rugged mountains, the sloughs surrounded with luscious grasses, the swamps filled with cranberries, co-existed with a rich dense growth of various kinds of trees. The woods were a fantasyland, a retreat - a refuge, freedom to wander and dream, to climb and race up and down those enticing mountains. It was where farmers gathered tall grasses, the hay, for their winter's supply. The abundance of trees provided the supply of firewood. Besides, there were berries, cranberries, strawberries, saskatoons and many others. How heavenly to wander through natures luxurious splendor, leisurely, slowly, enjoying the peace, the freedom, the beauty, alone with God's creation.

The vast area abounded in rich, lush grass and provided a rich pasture for the cattle. All summer long the cows were allowed to roam and graze freely during the day. There was one problem however. It was, at times, very difficult to find them in such a large area and bring them home at milking time. Sometimes the sound of the cowbell could not be heard because the herd had wandered too far. Sometimes it took hours to find them and bring them home.

It happened once that after searching high and low all day the family was ready to give up. We agreed to give it one more try - as a co-operative effort. So the whole crew, all five of us, sauntered along the path, enjoying the magnificent weather. It is quite probable that no one was overly concerned about the cows.

On either side of the path there was a dense growth of lush and tall trees. The growth was so dense that it was impossible to discern anything in it.

Suddenly we all stopped dead in our tracks. Some distance away there was a horrible racket. It was as if a whole regiment was storming a fortified barricade. There was crashing, pounding, roaring, trees falling, stomping, a regular earthquake!! It was most frightening. As usual Hélène knew what to do, she always did. "Sh, sh, sh," she cautioned, "perhaps our cows have met a strange herd and they are fighting. Be very quiet," she continued, "I will go on the other side of the bush and chase them out. If you stay here on alert we will surround them and drive them home!!" We were all a bit apprehensive, but it was so great that we had finally found the cows that we agreed. So Hélène sauntered cautiously around the bush and disappeared. We stood there waiting, hardly daring to breathe. We waited and we waited! And we held our breath not daring to make a sound. No Hélène. No cows! As scared as we had been before she left it now seemed inconsequential compared to the panic we felt for our sister's safety. "What could have happened to her?" we wondered. There was no sign of her or the cows. Besides, the noise had turned into a dead, eerie silence. Not a sound could be heard. Oh, we were silent alright, indeed we were! Even the sound of our breathing was fantasized as a threatening thunder. Time stood still indefinitely. At long last Hélène appeared on the far end of the bush. We breathed a sigh of relief. She was as white as a ghost! We all began in unison to ask the same question, "What happened? Where are the cows?" "Sh, sh," commended Hélène, walking or actually running away from that bush from which the racket had emerged. "But, but"...we insisted. "Be quiet!" she reiterated. By the horrified look on her face we began to think ruefully, "She must have seen a ghost, or maybe Lucifer himself! Only Satan could make that much racket all by himself." Finally when we had reached a safe distance from the ill-fated bush, she told us the whole story. "Scared, I was slowly and very cautiously getting closer and closer to the source of the commotion. I was sneaking up on what I thought were cows making an effort not to step on dead branches so that the herd would not be alerted and stampede. Suddenly I froze, for there right before my eyes and in the middle of that thicket was, not cows, but a man holding an axe, a team of horses tied to a tree. He was chopping frantically like a maniac, the trees crashing down everywhere beside him. At first he was unaware of my presence, but he must have sensed that someone was there, because he suddenly turned and saw me! It would have been beyond the bounds of possibility to judge which one of us was the most thunderstruck, him or me. He became rooted to the spot, his eyes bulging in disbelief. We both stood there speechless, staring at each other! How long? I haven't the faintest idea, but it seemed an eternity. What passed through that poor man's mind as he tried to unravel the absurdity of this freakish, outlandish encounter must have been extraordinary! I was the first to recover! In a flash I turned and like a bat out of hell I fled out of that bush as swiftly as my winged legs could fly! I had no way of knowing what this man was thinking, but to me those were the weirdest cows I had ever encountered!

It was obvious to my parents that the man had been gathering his winter supply of firewood. It was illegal to use any resources in the area without a permit. Making hay or felling trees for firewood required a license. But as money did not exist in most households, people made hay and cut firewood in spite of the law. They did this as secretly and surreptitiously as possible, hoping not to get caught. They had no alternative! The stock had to be fed and the homes heated during the brutal Saskatchewan winters.

Hence, the frantic and maniacal haste of the man to inconspicuously and rapidly cut a load of wood and return to his home unobserved. He probably thought my sister was a spy. Who knows!

My dad had an (almost) identical experience. He was making hay without a permit whenever the grass was luxurious encircling the sloughs. As he worked, he could hear the noise of another man's machine mowing the hay. One day the two met face to face. That evening he jokingly commented to my mother, "Well, I met my adversary today." "What did he say, what happened?" concerned, my mother asked. "Nothing, we just stared at each other without saying a word. I don't think he had a license either."

Jeannette Romaniuk

RELIGION

Again and again the crucial question surfaces in my mind, unsolved! What formidable compulsion enabled these noble souls to endure, to pursue undeterred this thankless path? Could it be that it was their strong, deeply embedded religious affiliation; a faith deeply rooted in their souls, unshaken throughout the generations. A faith that, beyond all this there is a power that transcends human understanding and imagination.

There is something mystical and radiant about the spiritual aspect of human life. It gives a new meaning to man's existence. It allows him to rise above, to transcend raw reality. No longer is life perceived as a struggle for mere survival, but as a journey of hope towards eternal peace and celestial happiness.

That inspiration and faith doubtlessly instilled in their hearts the courage and strength to continue on their grueling journey, never to falter in their quest. The belief in miracles and miraculous healing of terminal diseases, visions and celestial apparitions, events that have no scientific explanations accompany religious faith and traditions. Thus the moments of rejoicing emanating from their faith and strong conviction that it was all worthwhile must have sustained and upheld believers in their desperate struggle for survival. The traditions, the festive celebrations of religious holidays, the ceremonial aspects associated with and related to daily habitual routines connected with religious affiliation greatly enhance the quality and deeper meaning of life. These rituals engender a luster, an emanation from the monotony its tedious routine entails.

Christmas Eve and Christmas Day are surely the most dynamic, vivid portrayal of ceremonial religious holiday celebrations. The world is magically transformed by its mysterious and awe inspiring joy. Long ago, the breathtaking mysticism of this eventful day held our whole household enthralled. After months of preparations, the festivities began with the celebration of midnight mass. A cold seven mile ride in subzero weather to the church set the stage in the observance of the religious ceremony! The choirmaster was on her way to conduct the festive music for the joyful occasion. Warmly wrapped in every available blanket and seated snuggly at the bottom of the sleigh the whole family was gaily singing Christmas carols (in French), each one vainly gathering the snowflakes that were softly, gently falling. The crunch of the sleigh against the snow, the tinkling of the sleigh bells, the silence of winter created a mystical aura which only the imaginative fantasy of childhood can apprehend. It was a night of wonder, of illusive rapture.

Inside the church the festivities began. The violins (in harmonious parts) thrilled the melodious joy of the Christmas carols. The enchanting voices of the tenors in unison with the soprano and bass vocalists reverberated throughout the church, whose very foundation vibrated from their mighty resounding chant.

Here, there was no poverty, no deprivation, and no sadness. There was only the rejoicing of radiant spirits, an infinitesimal glimpse into the celestial kingdom of paradise as the voices of the choral group seemed to join the choir of the angels above. "Oh Holy Night" (Minuit Chretien).

The church was always elaborately decorated. Prominently displayed near the altar was the crèche, a miniature replica of our Savior's birth. This display was the delight of the younger members of the parish. They never left the church without contemplating it in every detail.

After the midnight mass everyone gathered at the grandparents' house for the "reveillon", an elaborate meal in the French Canadian tradition. Everyone was present. No one would have dared miss such a joyous celebration. There were uncles, aunts, cousins, brothers, sisters, mothers, fathers, children, babies, and of course the grandparents. The whole clan!

And, of course, every imaginable gourmet food was served. Grandmother's famous doughnuts "the tourtiere", turkey with all the trimmings, pies, cakes, Christmas pudding, fudge....

Everyone was celebrating! Singing, chatting and rejoicing in the love of one another's company. The memory of these Christmas Eve celebrations, "the reveillons", will remain forever treasured in my heart.

There were many other celebrations both spiritual and festive in nature. Easter to Christians has a deeper, more significant meaning than being merely a parade of Easter bonnets. To the ancestors it was a solemn, religious holiday. It was a celebration of the redemption and of Christ's Ascension into heaven. It was, like Christmas, accompanied with much rejoicing and festivities.

There were many other religious occasions that were justification for festivities and family gatherings. Baptisms, first communion, confirmation, a marriage. These special events when spiritually observed, instill greater meaning, and a deeper significance, than when observed merely with the superficiality of receiving and giving gifts.

The ceremonial aspects associated with daily routines were religiously observed. Family prayers were recited before retiring, and grace always preceded a meal. This spirituality complemented and promoted the cohesiveness and love for all the family members. It also created a respect for the gift of food - a meal became a special celebration. The strict observance of Sunday as the Lord's Day and attendance at church services was also a ritual. This seemed to create a deeper meaning to the essence of life itself. It not only seemed to create a respect for other individuals, but instilled a profound reverence for the self - the sanctity and the gift of "being". Suicide was an unheard of occurrence.

PROJECTS

When the farm failed to yield an adequate income sufficient to provide for their needs, the family pooled their ingenuity and resources together in order to examine and contemplate expedient means to resolve the situation.

Numerous enterprises were initiated and implemented. The schemes emanating from my mother's data bank were incalculable. The practicality of each of these schemes were meticulously examined and considered. Some were impractical at that particular time and place. Lack of capital, but mostly lack of transportation facilities, prohibited the feasibility of some of those enterprises. Nonetheless, one following closely on the heels of the last, the projects were launched, with a vengeance!

Where all these inspirations came from is beyond comprehension. Were they part and parcel of my mother's boundless imagination or her indefatigable determination to survive in impossible circumstances? But when one project failed or proved unprofitable another followed relentlessly and indomitably on its heels.

My father decided that the forest provided a far more profitable and viable source of income than the farm. Therefore every winter he proceeded to fill a railway tie contract extracted from its luxuriant supply. And there, within the glorious realm of nature was where his heart dwelt. It was for him the breath of freedom, the escape from the confines of barbwire barricaded captivity.

At the beginning of the 20th century the railroad companies were in the process of opening or constructing many railroad routes to provide services for outlying regions. The iron rails were secured on squared logs or ties. These logs were in great demand.

My dad managed to get a contract from Hetes and Sibald for this commodity every winter. He would establish his campsite wherever the trees were plentiful and mature enough to fit the required specifications of the product. He and my brothers worked in that area all winter leaving the campsite only to get provisions for themselves and feed for the horses. The entire procedure involved in the fabrication or construction of these "ties" was backbreaking labor. It was done by hand from start to finish. Power saws and skidders did not exist at that time.

First the trees were felled with a long, sharp edged and sharp-toothed saw called a crosscut saw. These saws were, according to my dad, magic! He claimed that when used by a skilled woodsman, the saw would literally zoom through the tree trunk unaided. And that the more pressure you applied to the ends the arduous the labor became.

After the tree was felled it was hued or squared on two sides with a sharp bladed, heavy tool called a broad axe. The treetop was left to secure the log while it was being hued. Then the log was cut or sawed in eight-foot lengths. A skilled worker managed to "square" sixty of these ties in one day.

The transportation of these logs (ties) proved to be the most problematic maneuver involved in the whole process. The ties were loaded on horse-drawn sleighs and taken to the nearest railway station. It was imperative that the hauling be done before the spring thaw. The sleigh's steel runners sliding on the frozen snow (ice) facilitated the movement and lessened the encumbrance of the load. In the event that the spring thaw occurred before the men were able to move the logs they used a most dangerous, antiquated and unwieldy method of transportation. Consequently it was seldom used, and then only when there was no other alternative. It was called the "drive". First the logs were skidded out of the woods. A heavy hook fastened them to a chain which was pulled by a team of horses unto a frozen river. Nowadays a skidder (a very efficient machine does this work). To propose skidding with horses to the modern generation would be at one's own risk, and I cannot guarantee the consequences (it would be a hazardous proposal at best).

The next step was the "drive". Apparently it was a most dramatic and exhilarating experience. In the spring, when the ice broke, the heavy current of the river floated the logs to the nearest train station. There they were loaded unto boxcars and transported by rail to the closest terminal and used in the construction of new railroad tracks.

The loggers had to be vigilant and needed a great deal of expertise when they followed the logs along the riverbanks. If the logs got tangled, in a jam, preventing the current from further movement, the loggers had to walk on the logs, wearing high rubber boots, and with a long sharp hook (a gaff) untangle them. The trick was to maintain one's balance and not fall into the ice cold water. Few men were capable of handling this task, as it was extremely dangerous. Especially when the current was swift and strong. The momentum and force of the entangled current-driven load could crush the fallen victim before being rescued. (From the innermost abyss of my memory tales of such tragedies seem to emerge). Looking back, it is almost unbelievable that each item was sold for one measly dollar!

In spite of the low remunerations, my father's expertise in assuming and fulfilling these winter contracts in the forest were always a continuous and reliable source of income. When a railroad contract failed to materialize, the men proceeded to sell pulpwood and firewood. This also never failed to replenish the meager family income.

My father remained forever enormously grateful for the experience, the skills, and the expertise he had gained in the lumber industry while working in Eastern Canada and the many states south of the border. It enabled him to make a substantial contribution to the support and welfare of the family.

The Blacksmith's Shop

The blacksmith's forge was another enterprise initiated in subsequent years. It was a brilliant idea! It was installed in an unused granary behind the house, the tools hung meticulously from nails on the wall.

Instead of traveling miles to the nearest town, the local farmers had minor repairs done right at their doorstep, so to speak. It was, however, used mostly to sharpen plough shares which was of course the service farmers needed most frequently. They came from far and wide to have their ploughshares sharpened. How fascinating to watch the red hot share come out of the coal fire unto an anvil and pounded with a heavy forge hammer until it was sharpened. It was exhilarating. This venture proved to be most profitable while it lasted. Unfortunately all the equipment belonged to my older brother, Jean. After he was established on his own farm he claimed and took what was rightfully his property.

Trapping

There was yet another project that must have been initiated in the very early years before the near extinction of fur bearing animals. Its memory lies many fathoms below in the deepest recesses of the mind, almost beyond the reach of the faintest recollection. To summon its spectral image and conjure up its hazy vision fraught with and entangled in cobwebs is to extend the memory beyond the confines of limitations. In that recollection my dad is cleaning, scraping the fat from the pelts of beavers, red foxes, weasels and minks. Then he is hanging them inside out on a frame to dry. A repulsive and nauseating sight.

Yet, though the picture is hazy, it is not an hallucination. Many of the local farmers went north during the winter months to trap these animals. The income derived from the sale of the fur brought a welcome supplement to the family's sparse budget. It was, indeed, another desperate attempt to replenish the inadequate farm revenue.

To many of these adventurers, trapping meant freedom. Their hearts rejoiced in the realm of nature's untrodden virginity.

An Untenable Project

In the thick of the depression, the family members pooled their ideas, frantically exploring any feasible (and even drastic) survival strategies.

On one occasion an ad appeared in the paper requesting a tutor for a family of children whose distance from school was prohibitive. Out of desperation my mother volunteered to fill that position. That decision caused a major upheaval in our household. The arguments pro and con raged through the nights, the whole family opposing such a drastic move. Yet it seemed a viable and temporary solution to a desperate situation. In spite of all this, the decision was in favor. It felt as if the anchor had suddenly been dashed from our ship, leaving it to drift into an uncharted sea. As if the whole bottom of the world had fallen out of our lives. Was $8.00 a month worth that much pain?

What happened to reverse that momentous decision is not clear. To the amazement and immense relief of everyone, she did not go. Perhaps someone prayed for a miracle!

The Cottage Industry

Next the family embarked on an enterprise which in England is defined as a "Cottage Industry". It imitated a wool textile factory. The raw wool was washed, dried, teased, carded, and spun into strands. Last of all it was knitted into woolen mittens, socks, scarves, sweaters...even underwear! These items brought rock-bottom prices. But it was a means of keeping the family together and the wolf away from the door.

Every family member was responsible for one of the procedures involved. My sister and I usually initiated the process by washing the raw wool (the filth and stench still makes me cringe, it was so disgusting). The teasing, which involved pulling the matted wool fibers apart after it was dried, was shared by all. It was my sister's choice to card or comb the wool. This was or is done with a tool called carders resembling a comb, but unlike a comb the teeth are constructed of wires. It disentangles the fibers, straightens them and faces them in one direction. This process prepares the fibers for the spinning wheel. My sister chose this task because it was the most difficult. She always assumed the most exhausting duties. She felt that her strength was superior to that of the rest of the family. She was amazing. In a later episode her contributions to the family welfare and well being will be narrated. Spinning the wool was my mother's department. Fine, delicate, medium, or coarse weave flowed expertly from that spindle. The average weave for men's stockings, mittens, scarves, sweaters, whereas the finer weaves were for ladies' delicate sweaters, gloves, berets and what-not... Some sweaters required the coarser strand for heavy winter wear. Dying the wool demanded scrupulous expertise and was relegated to the family's master craft woman, my mother, naturally!

The final stage, the knitting! Can the reader guess whose task that was? Why, the knitting machine, of course, me! Who else? Yes, who else could (or would) turn out a pair of mittens before breakfast and three knee high socks in one day? I never did live that reputation down! The male element of the family made sure of that. The constant tingling noise of the flying knitting needles preyed heavily on my overworked sister's nerves (and surely on everyone else's). Consequently it became imperative to retreat from the close knit circle of workers and seek the asylum at the farthest and most secluded corner of the room.

The project was reasonably successful. Customers were not lacking as the prices were more than reasonable. Double knitted mittens and knee-high men's' stockings sold for 75 cents. The sweaters? That has gone left field where all other forgotten memories dwell.

The reader may feel compelled to commiserate with the participants of this outlandish project. Wrongly so. It is not pity, but applause, that should be lavished upon such resourcefulness.

While seated in the performance of his/her particular task, something unforeseen, something deeper and spiritual was occurring. It was more than the response to a pressing need. It was a time when each in his/her own way shared the inner thoughts, feelings and essence of his/her soul. It was a time for discussions, story telling, study, and reflections. Sometimes the whole lot of artisans burst into a rollicking familiar song. The memory of sharing the mysticism and beauty of poetry still remains profoundly treasured in my heart. The rollicking songs gave momentum and animation to the enterprise in progress, whether it was work or play. A new burst of energy ensued from the euphoric, exhilarating rhythm, stimulating and invigorating it with renewed energy.

The western explorers must have felt the same enlivening and exhilaration as they rowed rhythmically to the beat of their songs, canoeing along the mighty, mysterious streams. The streams that led them into the unknown, the gateway to the west.

La Platform Cremelé

Years later, emanating from my mother's dramatic expertise, the family embarked on an exciting and daring (perhaps a little audacious) adventure. The birth of a dream had gradually become rooted in my mother's lavish imagination. Little by little it had been established and expanded until its realization appeared feasible. Her gift had been exploited but never utilized to her own self-fulfillment. Perhaps this bold plunge into such an ambitious, sensational enterprise was only the consummation of a beautiful dream. Or it may have been an intense desire to solve the severe economic crisis in which the family continually subsisted! Who knows! One day all caution was cast to the wind, "Cast your bread upon the waters," so the Holy Bible says, and that was what the family did. The great, great Herculean dream was launched...adrift into the great unknown, an unpredictable adventure.

To prepare for this courageous escapade the girls and one brother had meticulously rehearsed a theatre production, one in French and several English comedies. The French production was elaborate and may have been more suitable for an exclusive audience. It consisted of two musical attractions. The main play, entitled "Les Chausson de la Duchess Anne" and a musical comedy. Both plays were situated in Medieval France. The plot of the main attraction centered around the duchess's effort to retain her dominion over her dukedom. The intrigue, plus the suspense when a pair of slippers containing an urgent message is confused with some baked apple pastry in the shape of slippers (des chausson) keeps the audience guessing and completely absorbed in the plot. These "chaussons" were stolen by the Duchess's maidens and each confesses to the crime. The situation gets more complicated and ambiguous when the messenger also confesses to the crime. This confusion makes the play hilarious. The second play is about a "buffoon" who is lost in Paris and stops everyone he meets asking them to help him find his way. A family member was trained to accompany on the piano the vocalist who was performing on stage. Although home designed and fashioned, the costumes were magnificent.

The English production consisted of various hilarious comedies and was followed by providing the music for a dance afterwards.

It is obvious that performances in both languages were essential as in northern Saskatchewan some communities are entirely English speaking while others are entirely French. Besides, to reach a larger audience, half the proceeds were shared with the sponsors.

My dad was persuaded, with great difficulty, to construct a sort of covered wagon. It was spacious, comfortable, and was equipped with cubicles in which the props, costumes, and musical instruments could be safely stored. It was pulled by a team of horses. It was, also, heavy and unwieldy. The male element of the family nicknamed it "la platform cremelé" which has no English equivalent. The "lacy platform" may be the closest translation. The boys, of course, thought this hazardous venture was utterly out of this world.

The grand venture (the exodus) was launched. The performances were overwhelmingly successful. Everywhere it was performed the audience raved about the authenticity of the acting, the choice of the costumes and the meticulous manner in which the concert had been produced.

Years later while talking to a member of the cast an elderly lady was extolling the merits of the entertainment. She was, of course, unaware that she was speaking to someone who had actually participated and contributed to the excellence of the presentation.

But there was a problem. A problem that proved insurmountable! A truck, or a van, would have been required to carry such a volume of props, instruments, costumes and cast. The weight of the covered wagon and its contents was too demanding for the horses. They became exhausted and were unable to pull the strenuous load. The cost of a motor vehicle during the thirties was prohibitive. Discouraged, the family members had to return to their original professions and labor. All was not lost. It had been a memorable episode! (and a lot of fun!)

Besides all these resourceful enterprises, there was the incessant, astronomical garden project. The size of the vegetable portion, near the house, was reasonable and perhaps necessary. But the potato patch was immense. It stretched from the end of the garden to the far end of the field where the towering pine trees majestically stood.

My mother must have possessed the proverbial green thumb, for the vegetables emanating from that magic garden were luxurious, plentiful, and of a superior quality. These vegetables were an important source of food for the family. The corn and cucumber yields were especially abundant. Many evenings, when the house was full of guests, a boiler full of corn on the cob was cooked and shared. Barrels of dill pickles were processed for winter use. Besides providing an ample supply for the family, great bags of corn, cucumbers, carrots, and turnips were donated to our grateful neighbors. Extra vegetables were stored in a dugout or winter outdoor cellar. This was simply a deep and spacious pit. The vegetables were placed at the bottom of this pit and completely immersed or covered with sand. Then the pit was closed with a wooden cover upon which a thick layer of soil, straw and humus had been laid. This was, of course, to protect the vegetables from the frost. In the spring when the pit was uncovered the vegetables were garden fresh.

The potato patch was another matter. Probably part of the potato harvest was to be sold. Some years it was. But usually the patch yielded an overabundance. Storing the surplus was problematic. Some of the crop was stored in the cellar and some in the outdoor winter cellar. A great deal of the crop went bad as a result of the inadequate storage facility. This was not what concerned the younger members of the family. It was the responsibility of cultivating this enormous patch that irked them. Weeding and hoeing each row seemed an interminable task. These rows appeared endless. We beheld the tall pine trees at the far end of the field as a blessing. We couldn't wait to reach them. For there, at long last, we had finally completed the cultivation of one eternal row. For this import, the respite they provided from exhaustion, their refreshing shade, but especially their beauty, we never ceased to be grateful to that grove of imposing, stately pine trees.

That project had another crucial function besides procuring the nourishments for the family. It was a refuge where my mother could escape in the event of an insupportable situation. It provided her with a sanctuary where she could find peace, a space away from the "front". It was a retreat away from the incessant hubbub and constant pandemonium - the noise, the bickering, and the arguing, quarreling, etc.that crowded and confined living entails. The soothing arms of Mother Nature brought comfort and solace to her shattered nerves. In the deepest recesses of my memory bank a trickle flows along its slim cobwebs and brings back a picture to mind. It is a picture of pure bedlam! Work piled miles high over our heads and everyone wondering what to do next or how to handle such an impossible disaster and mother walking away, out the door! Then proceeding to the vegetable garden where she frantically began weeding and hoeing. The inexplicable question to an immature mind was "In the thickest of the fray, why is she abandoning us?" The answer is now glaringly evident. It has been replaced by a far more complex and formidable question. How did she not walk out that door, never to return? How was she able to come back to confront and resume the struggle? The answers to these are so intricate and unfathomable that it would bamboozle the minds of even the most capable and expert psychiatrist.

COMMUNITY

While reminiscing about the past and casting an overview of the neighbourhood, I finally realized what had always been dazzlingly conspicuous. The revelation that that backward glance unveiled before my eyes was astounding. The perception, the significance of its amazing enlightenment breathtaking! Not one in that diverse conglomeration of individuals had anything remotely in common with the other. Not only did they differ flagrantly in physical appearance, but in character and personality, they were at the opposite ends of the poles. And not only did they appear to emerge from extreme ends of the universe, but they seemed to have emanated from different species! It is beyond the imagination how such a hodge podge, pell mell divergence of individuals could be converged on one tiny speck of the earth's crust.

Perhaps it was the chicanery of fate for a laugh in its desire for diversion that amassed and dumped them all together, hit and miss, in one tiny, wee spot. There to dwell at the mercy of unpredictable destiny!

It is little wonder that the Quebecois insists on being distinct. Every single person in that little region was undeniably distinct - an island onto himself. Yet they all belonged to the same race and culture! Oddly enough that unique divergence in characteristic is what made each and everyone so exclusively extraordinary, so exciting, so amazing! Each could have been the subject of volumes. Every human character trait was represented. There was the domineering type with the tyranny of the lion versus the meekness as the lamb. There was the cunning of the fox versus the selflessness of Mother Theresa. There was the wisdom of Solomon versus the intellectually handicapped. There was the pessimist versus those who envisioned the world through rose-colored glasses, etc. Yet in their diversity, the people in the community rallied together and became one in times of need. They ignored or coped with their differences and pooled their talents, their goals and aspirations to become one whole.

A strong sense of community, a sense of belonging to something greater than themselves contributed to those pioneers' indefatigable, tenacious and relentless struggle against impossible odds. It was a feeling that bound them together as members of an extended family. What affected each member was the concern of the whole neighbourhood.

Success or misfortune was shared by all as brothers and sisters in a large household.

In the event of an epidemic neighbors shared medicine, knowledge, care, labor and even food. The whole community became one integral unit. This display of solidarity was never as unmistakable as during the crisis of the Spanish Flu. The whole community responded by pooling their resources in order to meet the needs of those afflicted with the disease. This catastrophic epidemic was so severe that no one (except my grandfather) was spared. Whole families lay unconscious for days on end. Parents, in some cases, were oblivious of the fact that their child lay dead beside them. Almost every household mourned the loss of a loved one. My infant brother, Paul Emil, died during the epidemic. My uncle Exihor was also taken. He was survived by a very young widow and four children.

It was during that most disastrous epidemic, the Spanish Flu, that providence manifested itself in the form of my grandfather and grandmother Savard. Characteristic of their magnanimous personality, they undertook the care of all those helplessly plagued by this merciless scourge. They, tenaciously and tirelessly, proceeded to go from house to house, performing any task necessary to alleviate the suffering of those afflicted. My grandfather, Francois, was the only one in the district who was mercifully spared. He went from neighbor to neighbor, feeding the animals, making sure that firewood was available to heat the homes (this was a major task in itself). Doing the chores as it was called. He was also the providential messenger responsible for bringing food and medicine to those stricken with the infection.

My grandmother became the angel of mercy. She had fortunately recovered from the disease two weeks before it struck everyone else. She was an expert in the care of the sick, using herbs and natural sources for medical supplies. In spite of the extent and severity of this contagious ailment she never faltered. With unflinching courage she went from house to house on her daily rounds.

The Spanish Flu crisis was not the first and only time my grandparents unselfishly came to the succor of those in dire circumstances. They had obviously dedicated their lives in the service of others. They lived by the teachings of our Lord who said, "Whatsoever you do to the least of my brothers, that you do unto me." For these magnanimous souls had a deeply embedded religious faith and lived by its teachings. Sunday mass was never missed. Lenten fast was strictly observed. Grace before meals, evening prayers, were always part of the daily ritual.

Their mission of mercy began long before they came west.

My Aunt Hélène apparently suffered from a chronic illness. She also had a most unhappy marriage. Perhaps her unhappiness contributed to the condition of her health and subsequently culminated in her death at a very early age. She was survived by three children, two boys and one girl, Bernadette. Although my Aunt Emma did help in providing and the nurturing of these orphans, the responsibility nevertheless for their care was assumed mostly by my grandparents. My grandmother's love for them was remarkable, especially for Bernadette. As she reminisced of these days long past, many were the tales she related about the humorous incidents that occurred while these children were with them. This incidence was one only among the innumerable and unknown others in which these providential angels rescued the needy. I deeply regret that most of the history of our loved ones before their arrival in the west remains buried in the past. Naturally, we are more aware and familiar with the events that occurred more recently and in closer proximity. Those are, of course, the events that occurred in the west.

In the northwestern part of Saskatchewan is where my grandparents resumed their mission of mercy. Their residence was a refuge for many who, for diverse reasons, found themselves in unfavorable circumstances. For instance, when my parents immigrated west, my grandparents' home was a welcome haven for them, until they were able to build a shelter of their own.

After the loss of her husband, during the Spanish Flu, my aunt found a well appreciated refuge with her parents. She was warmly received and provided with all her needs (along with those of her children) until she remarried a few years later. Religious instructions as a preparation for first communion or confirmation were given by the parish priest at the church. During these instructions all the grandchildren lived at their grandparents, as their house was much closer to the church. The children were then able to walk back and forth for their lessons.

There was besides the residents always one of the grandchildren visiting. Each child had a turn and spent a week with the grandparents. Perhaps it was during these weekly visits that the image of my uncle flashes back before my eyes as he whizzed through the evening prayers. My four cousins were apparently permanent visitors. They loved the peaceful and loving atmosphere the home provided and were reluctant to leave. The oldest, Maurice, especially seemed to feel at home there and refused to leave. This cousin was an absolute mechanical genius. He loved to tinker with the farm machinery, to my uncle's great exasperation. It may have been the tractor that fascinated Maurice so completely but it is very likely that Grandmother's scrumptious doughnuts had something to do with it. One day after he had downed a whole jar of them he turned to my Grandmother and said, "Your doughnuts are no good anymore, Grandma!"

The transients also often found shelter and refuge at my grandparents' home. They were those who had left home in search of employment. Disappointed in their search, many found themselves penniless and in dire circumstances. There were a considerable number of these. However only one of them has left an impression on my memory. He was called Mr. Montgolfier, appropriately indeed, as his whole deportment projected inflated extravagance, pure razzmatazz. His stature, however, did not do justice to his name, as he was barely four feet eight inches. What he lacked in stature nonetheless, he made up in personality. Thus he was indeed a giant, a virtual zeppelin when inflated. His pompous mien complemented by the eloquence of his speech, suggested grandeur of rank and stature. Some of his ingenious banter never failed to entertain his audience. Some of these will be resumed as the story progresses.

There were many who were rescued from want and destitution by my grandparents, too many to recall. The image of both grandparents will remain forever engraved in my memory. They are with those who tread in glory the other side of the unfathomable barrier that separates earth and the celestial kingdom.

In the following lines a glimpse is shed into the life drama of this extraordinary couple in order to pay tribute to them and to celebrate their cherished memory. My grandmother, Emeralda Savard, née Bouchard, descended from French nobility. Her great, great grandfather, the Duke of Seregeri (le Duke de la Seregeri) had two sons. The youngest son, thrilled by the sensational tales of the newly discovered lands, became obsessed with a feverish compulsion to seek his fortune in the "New World". The Duke, fearing for his son's safety, implored him not to venture such a hazardous sea voyage. The Duke's exhortations were in vain. In spite of the desperate father's threat that he would disown and disinherit him, the adventurous son embarked on the perilous journey. Arriving in what was then known as New France, the Duke's son participated in the early development of Quebec. At the time, in Quebec, the land was partitioned after the European system or manner. It was known as the feudal or seignorial system of land tenure. A seigneur was granted a vast track of land that was subsequently divided in long strips facing the St. Lawrence River. These strips were rented and cultivated by small farmers. Being of noble birth, it is likely that the Duke's son became a landowner, or seigneur. Nonetheless, having forfeited his title and his fortune, this ancestor was compelled to endure all the problems and rigors a newly developing country encounters. In the new world, the Americas, an Aristocratic or noble heritage was not revered as it was then in the European countries. It was (and is) the nobility of character that transcends all other personal traits or attributes, and nobility of character was what my grandmother, Emeralda, possessed. She was impervious to her noble heritage. What was of essence was the nobility of conduct. She was the embodiment of virtue and dignity. There was something fine, gentle, and refined about her. She projected such distinction and propriety that even as she sat in her long traditional dress, smoking her pipe with the men, she cast an aura of probity. She exalted grandeur and nobility even as she performed the most menial task on her tours of mercy. She undeniably belonged in a royal entourage!!! When my grandfather called, "Emeralda", everyone knew by the tone of his voice that he was calling a "queen", the queen of his heart!

Nonetheless, it was not this amazing woman's magnanimous charm and personality that endeared her so to the people's hearts, nor were these extraordinary qualities the reason why she was so popular.

When a malignant disease plagued the surrounding areas, or a contagious epidemic ravaged the neighbourhood, the whole community panicked with terror and desperation. Very few had any medical knowledge and therefore were incapable of caring for the sick. It was during these times of crisis that my grandmother came to the aid of those who had become afflicted. Like an angel of mercy, she diligently proceeded to alleviate the pain of those suffering in agony and fear. Those who witnessed her efforts regarded her as a providential angel who had come to deliver them of the diabolic cursed pestilence. Her expert medical knowledge and proficiency enabled her to treat the illness effectively and restore the patient back to health. Her tranquil and gentle manner brought comfort and reassurance to the patient. Her constant presence by the bedside, comforting and praying for healing, brought solace and peace.

Grandfather Francois Savard? Well, he was just great! "Great" is the only adequate term that becomes him. All six feet four inches of him, including his huge broad shoulders! His gigantic stature should have been intimidating to a child. On the contrary. His huge size was accompanied by a kind, vibrant, and cheerful personality.

There were rumors that he often exploded into violent outbursts of temper. He was also reputed as pacing indefinitely with his hands behind his back, talking to himself all the while, when facing a serious crisis or problem. But a child is blind to all these rumors. The benevolence, the righteousness of the loved one is all that matters. And to all his grandchildren he was the greatest. Just perfect!

Perhaps the most comical and endearing trait that great man possessed was his absentmindedness. He always seemed to be lost in deep contemplation. Consequently, he couldn't keep track of his belongings. Sometimes frustrated and extremely agitated, he would call,

"Emeralda! Emeralda! Where is my pipe?" Grandmother, always composed, would answer calmly, "Poor you, your pipe is in your mouth."

On other occasions, his mind wandering in space, lost in thought, he would point to whatever he needed or wanted at the dinner table. He wasn't being rude. It was just that he had drifted so far into his world of fantasy that he couldn't find his way back to reality. At least not on the spur of the moment. Everyone adored him so that whatever he did was considered appropriate, even righteous!

My grandfather's most striking attribute was his love and devotion for his family. He was first and foremost a family man. The interminable years he labored to provide for his loved ones, the priority he set on the excellence of his children's education, the manner in which he idolized his spouse, all corroborate the fact that the welfare of those dear to him took precedence over everything else.

Grandfather's sense of humor was what made him such an attractive personality. In fact that's what I liked the most about him. It was also what made him so popular with everyone, young or old. He teased (oh, how he teased!). He joked! He told tall tales and anecdotes of incidents that happened during his life. He talked about people with outstanding personalities he had met. He was particularly fond of recounting how one of his relatives, Elizabeth by name, had been the terror of the whole neighbourhood. She was known as "la bonne femme Elizabeth". She was regarded as a witch and approached only when it was crucially necessary and then with much trepidity, shaking in their boots. Perhaps she was not unlike the "shrew" in Shakespeare's "The Taming of the Shrew".

He listened with great enthusiasm and pleasure to stories told by someone else. He was hysterical with laughter when I told him how the waiter in Charles Dickens's "David Copperfield" had tricked David out of his meal and left the unfortunate timid boy starving. And when Grandfather laughed he would slap his knees and stamp his feet in pure delight. It was hilarious!

Perhaps it was Grandfather's looming, imposing and protective presence, combined with Grandmother Emeralda's gentility, that created a home from which emanated such peace and contentment. A home that was a sanctuary, a haven, an escape and reprieve from harsh reality. And all who in this abode did dwell, even temporarily, felt the aura of bliss in this congenial refuge and were reluctant, loathing the hour when the time would come to say goodbye.

Previous to the great exodus to the west, my grandfather had worked many years in the States. In Canada, upon the family's return, he worked at various jobs. He was in the crew of men who built the transcontinental railway across Canada. He was in the group of men when the last spike was driven at the end of the line. Therefore he was instrumental in building the west. During those long, weary months away from home, my grandfather longed to be with his family. His acute loneliness was intensified when he received letters from my grandmother. These letters were filled with the latest news concerning the family. Grandfather was, to his great distress, unable to read or answer my grandmother's letters. The educational opportunities at the beginning of the 19th century were practically non-existent as children were compelled to contribute to the support of the family. The fact that he could not communicate with his family was, to my grandfather, unbearable. So he determined that he would learn to read and write. Late at night, in spite of the fatigue after working long hours on the railroad, he studied endlessly, undaunted by the difficulty of the enormous task he had set for himself. After many grueling hours, and Herculean effort, he managed miraculously to teach himself to read and write in both languages, English and French. He was now able to correspond with his family. He could also read the newspaper. But the most startling result was that he became the railroad crews' secretary. The other members of the crew, equally longing for their families, were ecstatic that they could at last get news from their loved ones.

There were other generous and magnanimous residents in that community. Many others performed unlimited contributions to the welfare and benefit of their neighbors. In times of distress and urgency, these benevolent folk never refused aid to those in need.

There was an English family, the Nobles, in the vicinity who lived about a mile from our house. They also were unlike any of the other individuals in the region. But, like my grandparents, they were "angels of mercy" or a replica of the "Good Samaritan". Regardless of the need they were there. Transportation, food, medicine were always shared generously with anyone in need. It is impossible to estimate the number of trips to the doctor or to the hospital this compassionate man made in response to an emergency.

It is also impossible to imagine how many times the children in our household were sent to borrow one thing or another from these good people. The term borrowing was a dirty word in our house, synonymous to begging. How we loathed these "borrowing" errands.

Apparently that family was more affluent than their neighbors. They owned an automobile, which was exceptional for the times. There were only two farmers who could afford one, the Nobles and my Uncle; all others traveled in horse drawn buggy or vehicles. Evidently it was because they owned the only means of rapid transportation that they were able to help in cases of extreme emergency. My sister and I were trying to complete our high school education through the Department of Education Correspondence School. We could not afford to buy the textbooks required to accompany the lessons. The youngest son, Walter, having completed his grade twelve, lent or gave us all the books that were needed. We are, and were then, eternally grateful for his generosity.

Thus even during the trials of the early years many settlers opened their doors to those less fortunate than themselves. Our home was no exception.

The natives took refuge at our humble home because they needed shelter from the bitter cold. They needed rest and food. But they were not the only ones. Traveling long distances in a horse drawn vehicle was incredibly exhausting. Many would stop to feed and water their horses. Meanwhile they would enjoy a much needed respite from the fatigue of their journey. This act of lending a hand to someone in need was, of course, what any human being would do.

But it did not end there. My mother had an obsession, a compulsion to aid the destitute and rescue those in trouble. The most incredulous thing about this extraordinary woman was her ability to transform nullity into reality. It is positively unfathomable how she managed to do this; but manage she did! She managed to find the wherewithal to feed and open her door to anyone who came knocking. Did she, like Jesus, have the power to multiply the loaves and the fishes? Quite unlikely. Nonetheless, during the "dirty thirties" when everyone existed on precariously little, my mother continued her indefatigable quest. She transformed her home into a sanctuary. "Give to those in want a glass of water and you shall receive a barrel" was her dictum.

During the depression, many young men, in an effort to seek employment, wandered away from their homes. They were often unable to find work and found themselves in very unfortunate situations. Without money, food or shelter, they faced a very grim prospect.

One of these young men, Charmand, a handsome, blond, gallant strayed over to our house one day. He was a charmer. His dashing personality, his grace on the dance floor, and his seducing voice, mesmerized all the ladies in his entourage. Unfortunately Charmand was convinced that his charm was the access to success and plenty. Earning a living was too menial and degrading a task for such a flamboyant personage. He claimed he was seeking employment but secretly prayed that he would not find any. He stayed indefinitely wherever he was welcomed until it was quite plain that he had overstayed and imposed on his host's generosity. He left only to impinge on someone else's hospitality.

There was another young man who stayed at our house. This young man, unlike Mr. Charming, was very responsible. He would not take advantage of anyone's generosity or "mooch". Unfortunately he had a violent temper. This trait was the cause of a great deal of anxiety and problems in later years. Regrettably, he was lured into a card game one evening. There were four players and they were playing in a shed or barn. One of the gamblers was apparently more cunning than the others and succeeded in winning all the money. It goes without saying that those who were swindled out of their last penny were not very happy. After the game all of them left, except the winner. He had borrowed a horse to come to the game and was in the process of mounting his horse to leave. One of the men came back, perhaps to demand his money. There was a violent fight. The outcome was tragic. The man who had won all the money was murdered with a fork. All those who had been at the game became suspects and were continually under surveillance. They were constantly harassed with endless questions by the police, who were trying to solve the crime. Years later, on his deathbed, the culprit confessed his guilt. But it had cost the other players years of terror, living in fear that they might be held responsible for a crime that they did not commit besides having to bear the torment of being incessantly harassed by the police. Even though these men were innocent, they knew that sometimes circumstantial evidence can be pretty damning. The Hildegarde case bears conclusive evidence to that fact.

Besides harboring all these homeless, transient, unemployed youths, we had practically adopted a whole household, "Les Beautemps". The entire family, with the exception of the very young children, lived at our house. They were accepted and treated as permanent members of the household. There was a sort of unspoken understanding that these guests would help with the chores, or whatever had to be done, in order to compensate for their food and lodgings.

They had the very best of intentions. Willingly and cheerfully they always did what had to be done, to the best of their ability! But work was a concept completely alien to them (it was not in their job description!!). Even the simplest task always turned out to be astronomical, even Herculean. For instance, one morning when the men were preparing to go north to work, one of the boys, Wilson, was requested to go and cut a hole in the ice on the lake so that the farm animals could have water to drink. Upon his return he had this dejected look. It was evident that something was not right. "What's wrong?" my dad asked. "There is no more water in the lake," he replied, "it has gone dry!" "Well, that is indeed very strange," said my dad. "I have lived here for twenty-five years and there has always been plenty of water in that lake. It has never shown any sign of drying up." "I dug and dug," Wilson went on, "but couldn't get any water. Not a drop." The poor boy looked so wretched that, in spite of his haste to get on his way, my dad went to the lake and easily got water for the animals.

On another occasion, the men were again preparing to leave early so that they would arrive at the work site before sunset. They still had to get potatoes from the cellar. The oldest of the boys, Carl, (there were three of them) was asked to help fill a bag with the potatoes. Well...with one hand he would grab a potato and slowly...ever so slowly...put it in the bag. My dad was exasperated. "At least," said he, "use both hands." It had never occurred to him to do so! It is quite likely that every one of us, henceforth, proceeded to do whatever had to be done, as help was not forthcoming.

And there was a lot to be done. Just the preparation of meals for so many was an enormous task. And the cleaning after the meals, washing dishes, etc. took hours, as dishwashers did not exist at the time. There were as many, and sometimes more, guests seated at that table, as there were members in the family. Fortunately we had a huge homemade table. There was never an empty space around it. Yet no one ever left the table hungry.

Although our adopted family did not possess the skill necessary to earn their living, they possessed other gifts. They were artists! From the oldest to the youngest, they were entertainers. They were all violinists and were able to play any other instruments within their grasp. And dance! Wow! Their ability to follow and beat the rhythm was uncanny! The father, not musically inclined, was not to be outdone. He could spin a yarn the likes of which could make your hair stand straight up on ends. And joke! His stories were hilarious! Indeed, he was the only person who could make my dad laugh heartily. Mrs. Beautemps strutted around, a veritable peacock (penniless) as if she owned the whole world. And so she did! She possessed the most priceless of treasures, happiness! Her entire household played, danced, and sang from morning till night. Their exuberant joy compensated for their hunger and they forgot all about their empty stomachs. They were the most perfect personification of the cricket in Lafontaine's "La Cigale et la Fourmi". They most likely lived according to this passage in the Holy Bible. Luke 22: "Do not be concerned for your life, what you are to eat, or for your body, what you are to wear. Consider the ravens: they do not sow; they do not reap - yet God feeds them. How much more important you are than the birds - or take the lilies of the field: they do not spin, they do not weave; but I tell you Solomon in all his splendor was not arrayed like any of them. Why toil and fret when abundance is being lavished upon you." That was the message that the family wanted to impress upon their neighbors, supposedly! In the fierce struggle (rage) and frenzy to accumulate the so-called necessities of life, we by-pass and ignore the only thing we really need, happiness! They had and cherished what all are seeking and most will never find: the precious gift of happiness.

Had they lived in modern times, with modern facilities, the family would undoubtedly have become famous and wealthy. Unfortunately they lived in the wrong place at the wrong time. The crucial question is: Would they have been happier had they become famous and possessed all the wealth in the world? One wonders! Sometimes simplicity and moderation far surpasses complexity and extravagance.

The wooden breadbox between the cupboards often conjures the memory of Sam Mongolfier. He was indeed a colorful character, although less than five feet tall. Nonetheless, what he lacked in stature he made up in personality and thus he was indeed extraordinary. The first flashback of Sam is comical. He is standing in front of the breadbox where he always sat as soon as he entered the house. He is madly tugging at his trousers, greatly agitated. "Oh, but scrap that thing at once. Throw it in the junk pile right now." He keeps repeating on and on while still tugging at his trousers and staring at the clock. Even before greetings are exchanged! No one knows what he's talking about. No one can even guess why he is so flustered. Everyone just stares at him!

Finally it dawns on everyone that his agitation is caused by the clock which is ten minutes slow. He finally calms down and sits on his favorite seat, the breadbox. This M. Sam's image keeps flashing back in my memory. Unique and distinct he most certainly was. He often visited our house for various reasons. Sometimes just to tell tall tales and exchange small talk. He often came to cut everyone's hair, for he was the community's local barber. Although he had had no training he was an excellent hair stylist and there was a great demand for his services. Notwithstanding his popularity he did not prosper. It is not surprising! He charged the fabulous amount of 25 cents per hair cut. On one occasion he bought the two older girls in the family expensive and fashionable hats to go to church. At the time ladies were not allowed to enter the church without wearing a suitable hat.

There was a rumor that Sam was quite a penny pincher - a veritable Scrooge. Neighbors dropping in at mealtime were never invited to share his fare or to join him for a meal. To prove this for himself, a friend decided to drop in on Sam at mealtime. As he was not being invited to partake of the meal, the friend decided to wait and find out if Sam would eventually break down and offer him something to eat. He waited five whole hours! No nourishment was forthcoming. The friend had to leave without being fed. Sam's reluctance may have been that being a bachelor he did not feel that his cooking was good enough for visitors. He therefore was obviously hesitant to serve it.

In his declining years, Sam gave refuge to a lady who had a small daughter. His frugal means and lifestyle was unacceptable and insufficient to provide for a lady with a child. She soon left to find greener pastures.

It is most gratifying to know that after the lady left, someone came to live with Sam. That person took care of him during his last days. He also took care of all financial and funeral arrangements.

Sam's unique, idiosyncratic personality never failed to bring laughter and merriment to all whom associated with him wherever he went. He was always a welcome guest at our house. Everyone enjoyed his jokes and banter.

A Most Regrettable Loss

In the parish choir were two tenors, Mr. Rossignol and Mr. Beauchant, whose majestic alluring voices singing the liturgy of the mass enchanted the entire congregation. The swaying resonance of their chant pulsated softly and reverberated gently throughout the shrine, mesmerizing all within its walls.

Excepting for the majesty and beauty of his voice, the life drama of Mr. Beauchant is unfamiliar to me. He lived in a nearby district, quite a distance from our house.

Mr. Rossignol was the husband of the postmistress. The post office was in the immediate neighbourhood, consequently the family was well known. The postmistress Mrs. Rossignol, a very proper, dignified lady, performed a most valuable service for the community. Seated at her desk facing the mail cubicles Mme Rossignol efficiently, competently sorted the mail for a large rural area. Her services were greatly appreciated and she was well respected by all. Many were somewhat intimidated by her meticulous, undeviating conformity to explicit details. Yet, all the local residents were immensely grateful for the indispensable function she performed for them. For in rural areas the mail was regarded as sacred. It was the only liaison the people had with the rest of the world. In modern times it would be unimaginable to exist without access to various means of communication. Televisions, radios, computers, fax machines, telephones are deemed vital requisites for mere survival. But then people looked forward to letters and newspapers with eager, anxious anticipation. The local residents could not wait to get the mail from one mail day to the next.

It would have been undeniably difficult to judge which of that admirable couple was most appreciated in the community. Mrs. Rossignol performed a daily service for everyone, whereas her husband's contribution was only on Sundays. But the ecstasy, the rapture that magnificent melodious voice brought was incomparable.

Were it not for this remarkable gift this man would probably have remained unnoticed. For he was an unassuming, self-effacing and gentle person. He was always invisible when people came to pick up their mail. It is indeed fortunate that he made such an extraordinary and formidable impression on Sundays - as regrettably no one would have known he existed.

The task of cultivating the land appeared incompatible to Mr. Rossignol. It seemed inconsistent with his nature. The confines it imposed restricted his yearning for the freedom of the unbarricaded wilderness. The beckoning of the vast expanses lured him incessantly.

When winter frost came and snow covered the land he would set off into the forest to trap fur bearing animals (and perhaps to dream). There he could savor the freedom he had longed and yearned for throughout the interminable days of summer.

One year early in the fall before the rivers and lakes were frozen, Mr. Rossignol, a friend Mr. Bonneau and his son, decided to travel north by canoe. As soon as they arrived at the intended site, they built themselves a cozy log cabin, settled themselves comfortably, and made preparations to trap all winter.

Unfortunately, soon after their arrival Mr. Rossignol became ill. His illness was so severe that his friend spent all his time caring for him. It was impossible to go for help as the rivers were frozen solid and their only means of travel was by canoe. Night and day Mr. Bonneau anxiously and desperately cared for his friend. Lacking the necessary medication and expertise it was a hopeless situation. Regrettably, Mr. Rossignol passed away. Overcome with grief, and isolated in the grip of winter's merciless jaws, the father and son had no choice but to bury the deceased in the northern wilderness.

Besides the anguish over the loss of his friend, Mr. Bonneau was frantic with concern about the mental condition of his son. Unaccustomed to the isolation of the north, this ill-fated lad's loneliness was driving him totally to the point of insanity. The merciful spring thaw must have been anxiously awaited by both father and son.

Years afterwards, Mr. Rossignol's eldest son endeavored to find his father's burial site. He intended to bring the body home for a proper burial ceremony and place him in the cemetery. The search was futile.

This may be a misconception, but judging from his aspirations, this kindly man is where his heart forever longed to be. The magnificence of nature surrounds him and holds him in the splendor of its bosom. He is home; free at last! Oh, that he should be left in peace to rest.

The cabin built by the trio still stands and is often used as shelter by firefighters, search parties or sometimes by someone who has lost his way in the woods. It is named after the one whose spirit resides within the magic realm of the virgin and untamed wilderness.

Whenever the memory of this noble man manifests itself in my thoughts, a message to his spirit miraculously gushes out of my heart. It is a message that is humbly written as a eulogy and in memoriam of his noble and faithful life.

Dear Mr. Rossignol, let the vibrations of your melodies pouring forth from your noble heart, so shake the portals of heaven's gates that they will burst open with the joy felt in the magic of your canticles (psalms). Let the choirs of heaven acclaim you as you were once welcomed in the hearts of all the parishioners that most fateful day of the Lord. You, in the pursuit of your dreams; dreams full of beauty, magnificence and glory, were led to an unmarked, unknown grave hidden in the arms of your beloved virgin nature.

Perhaps nature's garden continues to be a manifestation of the rapture emanating from your noble heart.

Jeopardy (Choir in Peril)

So far, the reader may have had the impression that the neighborhood in the district where we lived was teeming with saints. But you may have been grossly misled. The truth is that it was teeming with individuals who were infested with idiosyncrasies. And these eccentricities were what made each one of them so unique, intriguing, beguiling!!! And at times even hilarious!

Let's begin by contemplating someone who thought he was sitting on top of the world like a peacock, preening his glamorous feathers, Mr. Paon.

This gentleman had uncompromisingly, tenaciously and irrevocably resolved to join the vocalists in the church choir. All things being equal, this decision should have been favorable, but as it turned out it proved to be a disaster.

Because of her superior musical ability and talent my mother played the piano in the church choir. She was also responsible for training, directing and accompanying the vocalists. The selection of suitable candidates was often a problem. The choristers had to possess a smothering of musical talent or at least have the ability to sing in tune, and maintain a melody without straying into dissonance.

The parish was blessed with two male tenors, Mr. Rossignol and Mr. Beauchant, whose voices were powerful and heavenly to behold. They led the other members of the choral group with their true melodious voices.

This gentleman, a parishioner, sought to elevate himself in the eyes of his neighbors by being a member of this choral group. He was tone deaf. Absolutely, irrevocably tone deaf! Yet he insisted on singing with the rest of the vocalists! Every Sunday he strutted up to the choir loft and bellowed out his renditions of the canticles. This, on most occasions, was not irreparable, as the tenors, with their majestic voices, either kept him on track or drowned out his false discordant performance.

One Sunday, however, disaster struck! Neither one of the tenors was present. Alas the mass had to begin! To my mother's dismay, Mr. Paon intoned the "Kyrie". Oblivious to the accompaniment and support of the organist, he strayed further and further in spatial discord. No matter how violently the organist shook her head and shrugged her shoulders, our unfortunate hero kept straying deeper and deeper into the very abyss of dissonance and discord. To my mother, who could not tolerate a false note, it was as painful as a dagger piercing her ears. At last he knew that he could never hope to extricate himself, he had wandered too far off track. The congregation held its breath and cringed with embarrassment. For such a flagrant misdemeanor against the reverence and sanctity of Sunday mass celebration was regarded as sacrilegious.

Suddenly the doors of the church burst open! A majestic, thunderous voice boomed throughout the church. It's very foundation shook and even the walls rattled with the magnitude of the vibrations. Kyrie Elieson... An answer to a prayer! Salvation in times of crisis! Disaster averted. Mr. Rossignol, our tenor, had again saved the day with his powerful voice. The congregation breathed a sigh of relief, thanking God for his many mercies (not the least of which was to rescue and deliver the Kyrie from the onslaught of a peacock). They had been rescued from an unforgettable calamity, the humiliation and tragedy of sinking into the pit of dissonance!

That episode was, to the members of the choir, the breaking point. "That does it!" they protested, "Something must be done about this 'Caruso'. He renders it impossible to maintain a true melodious air while he bellows out of tune." As usual, my mother was elected to "do something". She approached the parish priest and asked for his counsel and recommendations in solving this rather delicate situation. This saintly man, however, would, under no circumstance, intentionally hurt anyone's feelings. "Well," said he, "this is a sensitive matter indeed. It is imperative that we do not hurt this man's feeling or demean him in anyway. Therefore the situation must be handled tactfully and thoughtfully." "But," responded my mother, "he has had numerous insinuations and polite suggestions that he is unable to participate in the group because he lacks the musical facility it demands. The Kyrie episode at mass on Sunday should have irrevocably convinced even him of that fact." "My dear lady," continued the priest, "you will never convince this man that he does not possess the talent to sing at the Sunday mass. He will be insulted if it is even suggested to him. He is either incognizant of the fact or he denies it even to himself." "So," said my mother, "we are fighting a hopeless battle." "Not only for that reason," replied the priest, "but you know that this person is one of us, and belongs to the richest family in the parish. Their generous donations support the church. Most of the parishioners' contributions are negligible compared to theirs. The church depends on their support. Spiritually the crucial issue is not, and does not, have anything to do with money, but remember," continued the gentle priest, "that the gifts to the Almighty are strictly contingent upon those that the Lord has bestowed upon them."

A quotation taken from a hymnbook says, "I am poor, but I have brought myself the best I could." Surely this is expressed in that man's performance. "I am tone deaf, but I sing the best I can. Please Lord accept my gift."

Who could refute or even question the wisdom of the wise old priest's words. So ended the dream of finding a solution to the choristers' dilemma. There was nothing to do but to pray that the majestic voice of our tenors would prevent utter chaos in the vocalist's section during the celebration of the Sunday masses.

Our two heroes, Mr. Beauchant the tenor, and Mr. Paon the singer, had another confrontation. It was on the occasion of a church picnic. As usual, my mother had organized the whole affair, which included many diverse events. Competitions, games, races, horse races were included. All in all it was a fun day. It was, that is, until the horse races event.

Mr. Beauchant and Mr. Paon both entered their prize horses in the race. Mind you, these horses were not thoroughbred. But in the eyes of the owners, they were even more precious. At any rate the two horses, Mr. Beauchant's and Mr. Paon's, competed against each other. The winner, unfortunately was Mr. Paon's horse. Mr. Beauchant insisted that Mr. Paon's horse had won by foul play. His powerful voice thundered throughout the grounds accusing the perpetrator of cheating in no uncertain terms. "You cheated, you are a dirty low down thief!" he screamed (these words still echo in my ears after all these years). The intimidated crowd froze in suspense. Would this wonderful day end in a fight? Someone must have acted as a mediator because both men were placated and went home. The festivities resumed peacefully. The excess ice cream was donated to the children. Scraping the sides of a five gallon container they smacked their lips with pure delight - Hum-m-m-! Never had anything tasted so sumptuously delicious. I can still taste its luscious flavor. Pure rapture! Never again did ice cream bring such delight!!!

Theatrical Performances (to amass funds for the church)

The teachers at the private schools devoted a large portion of the scholastic time and effort to the arts. They concentrated on the development of musical and dramatic expertise. The monumental advantages this "savoir faire" brought to the lives of their students far outweighed the sacrifices they incurred. It enhanced the quality of the students' lives, enabled them to dwell into depths of rapture and ecstasy previously unknown. It brought them the admiration and esteem of their peers. At any social function they were the center of attraction, the life of the party. But the retreat into a tranquil, soothing haven, an escape in times of stress, surpassed all these.

Thus upon graduation many students were accomplished musicians and possessed the expertise to follow a musical career. Some, like my aunts, did. Many graduates were qualified and capable of producing and directing theatrical performances and concerts. It was in this field that my mother directed and expanded her expertise and her energy.

This expertise turned out to be monumentally efficacious not many years later during the dirty thirties. For once, the ramifications of the cursed depression may have been advantageous to someone. The scheme that originated as a result of the stringent consequences of this scourge provided an opportunity for the manifestation of my mother's outstanding leadership, organization, and resourceful abilities. It provided an outlet for the expression of her extraordinary musical and dramatic talents.

The scheme itself was a desperate and urgent attempt to amass funds exigent to the support of the church. A theatrical performance was to be produced and the proceeds were to be used for the church's benefit.

The source of this inspiration is unmistakable. Doubtless it emanated straight from the wisdom of the convent teachers (the nuns) journeying directly through the "savoir faire" they had inculcated in one student's brilliant mind.

It was indeed a monumental enterprise. To organize, in a rural setting, and successfully manage such a huge undertaking, it was critical that the director-producer possess the required qualifications, experience and talents.

My mother, confident that the project might partially solve the church's economic crisis, had made the suggestion. Besides, she was the sole individual in the parish who possessed the qualifications, the talent and determination to even attempt such a gargantuan venture. So she was chosen and saddled with the operation of the whole project, from A to Z. This was, of course, not what she had anticipated. Undeterred my mother proceeded to set the project in motion. The initial step was to convince and persuade the parish priest of the practicality, the feasibility and the anticipated success of the venture. Next, the stage in the church basement, where the performance was to be held, had to be equipped with adjustable curtains and essential props suitable for the production.

The selection of the plays and acts for the performance did not present any problems. Of these, there was an unlimited, plenteous source in the bountiful repertoire of my mother's phenomenal imagination.

Perhaps the most horrendous, formidable task in the difficult production of a performance was choosing the performers, especially in a rural area. The characters (actors) were chosen at random and most had little ability. Often the cast lacked the education and refinement essential for and to assume the role of the characters in the plays. Besides, the choice of players was a very delicate matter. It was impossible to refuse individuals who volunteered for a part or role without appearing prejudicial and creating negative public relations.

Consequently, with a cast consisting of individuals of little or no talent and lacking dramatic aptitude, the preparation and training period was grueling. It demanded infinite hours of rehearsing, coaching, teaching, repetition night after night in the hope of some degree of excellence. In some rare occasions providence would send an individual who was the exact embodiment of the desired character.

Many times unable to achieve the desired results, she would assume a role that was especially difficult or demanding. That woman (my mother) had an incredible flair for drama. She could impersonate any character with ease, whether it be female or male. Any character, a queen, the peasant woman, the clown, and especially the comedian. Indeed she portrayed the comedian with such enthusiasm that the audience was swayed into believing that she was the real character. The male role was a problem as she was a mere 5'1" tall, but instead of detracting, it seemed to create a credible, hilarious effect.

She also possessed a knack of improvisation, compensation, and the ability to make adjustments in order to achieve the desired results. The art of improvisation often required specific skills. For instance, the ability to make an illusion appear a reality. This was imperative in the production of a musical performance. Many individuals were unable to sing. They were either unable to project their voices effectively or were tone deaf. My mother compensated for this by hiding behind the curtains and singing for the player on stage, who pretended to be the vocalist. The audience was apparently unaware of the improvisation. The performances were often a disappointment, however, and failed to achieve the goal of excellence she had anticipated. Nonetheless the performances must have had some merit and audience appeal as my mother was implored to produce other spectacles year after year, both for entertainment, and to amass funds for charitable purposes.

My memoirs are filled with the production of these theatrical performances. Some flashing visions involve the rehearsals. The actors usually gathered at the house and the practices were held among the ongoing commotion of the household. There were the interminable repetitions of the lines and gestures until some semblance of the desired effect had been attained. This involved countless skills such as emotional expressions, mannerism, intonation and voice production... The producer demanded perfection in order to attain the quality and the effect desired.

Other visions are of the actual stage performances. These were dramatically successful and had great audience appeal, yet they failed to meet my mother's criteria of excellence.

News (Plus!)

Small, closed communities have little need for daily newspapers, radio or television. At that period of time at any rate. News and events concerning the neighbourhood are more efficiently covered by local gossip.

In the community where we lived a central broadcasting system existed, especially in the person of one charming lady (correction: there may have been several that were unknown). This lady made it her duty to spread any event in the locality, especially if the event was a little juicy or shady. She relished these and made sure no one ignored every minute detail of its contents. It was a well-known fact that if someone wanted to advertise something, all that was necessary was to tell this good lady. But woo if "the something" was to be kept confidential.

The pandemonium these stories caused in this neighbourhood were hair raising. They were probably a welcome relief from the monotony of the daily humdrum routine. There were little distractions and forms of entertainment. Farmers lived considerably far apart and there were few visitors. Movies and the theatre were non-existent. There were of course local dances for the young people. Older folks played cards or chatted when visiting at their neighbor's house. Some found joy in the beauty that nature has so lavishly displayed for all who are fortunate enough to live far away from the confines of city life.

Each person, according to his own individuality, resorted to his own way of enjoying any precariously little leisure time available to him.

A Most Grievous Misfortune

My sister Juliette had very little luck with employers. At fourteen she worked for an overbearing M. LeDroit. This man reigned with an iron hand over his household. His unfortunate spouse had no voice in making any decisions regarding the management of the business, the employees, or even the household. She had given up that right ages ago. The employees were expected to work from sun up till all hours of the night with minimum wages. Even then, he was never satisfied and expressed it in no uncertain terms. "Young people today are useless," he complained in his loud, imperious, domineering voice, "They are incompetent and a drain on their employers." Strangely enough he never complained about my sister Juliette's ability to earn her wages. Indeed that may not be surprising as she was capable and performed her duties expeditiously and efficiently well.

Part of Juliette's duties consisted of outdoor chores; the care of farm animals, etc. She was assisted in this task by a gentleman who was a diabetic. One day, in the wee hours of the morning just before dawn, she hurriedly entered the stable to help feed the animals and milk the cows. To her horror, her assistant was lying motionless; face down in the alley that separates the rows of stalls in the middle of the barn. Thinking that he had just fainted or perhaps tripped and had been unable to regain his composure, Juliette tried desperately and hopelessly to revive him. At last, when her efforts failed, she panicked. Instead of running back to the farmer's house she literally flew to a neighbor's house 'Good Sam', who was a close friend of the family. This dependable friend immediately proceeded to M. LeDroit's stable, and as he anticipated, found that the poor man had passed away from an insulin injection. The farmer was alerted and he took charge of the situation. Juliette, however, could not be persuaded or convinced under any circumstance to remain at the sight. She was taken home. For months, or perhaps years, following this tragic episode, the vision of this man lying on the floor of the stable haunted her. The specter followed her wherever she went. One of us had to accompany her even across the room to get a drink of water. It must have been a horrifying ordeal! The story of this man's (M. LeDroit) ramifications upon the lives of other people does not end there however and should be told.

The couple was childless for fourteen years following their marriage. This was, indeed, a blessing as "His Righteousness" thought children were a burden. The wife, well, no one knew (if she wanted children or not), as the expression of her feelings and happiness were prohibited in that relationship.

As fate would have it, after all these years, a son was born to them. Instead of being overjoyed as most parents are at this blessing, the father was devastated. At the child's baptism he insisted on naming his son "Calamity". "Be merciful," pleaded the priest, horrified, "do not condemn this child to a name, a shadow of doom, that will haunt him forever, for Calvin would be more appropriate and not so abominable." "So be it," retorted the irate father, as he stormed out of the house.

Years afterwards, upon returning to the neighborhood, I was told that the couple had several other children. And one wonders, "Did this implacable man have a change of heart or did he manifest the same merciless inhumanity towards the others?"

It was also rumored that after years of remaining in this miserable relationship, the ill-fated Mme LeDroit's life ended in tragedy. May her soul rest and rejoice in the peace and freedom (that were so grossly denied her on this earth) in the sanctuary of the celestial kingdom where she now dwells.

Deprivation?

Another entrepreneur in the local agricultural field was a certain Mr. Bredouille. This man was an island unto himself. The whole farming business seemed to be a mystery. To him it was an illusive maze in which he could not find his way in or out. It appears that he couldn't figure out what was to be done next in the operation and management of the whole affair (the financial and bookkeeping aspects must have been gargantuan). Most experienced farmers know when it is time to plant and harvest their crops. They know that the weatherman is an inflexible, unrelenting and temperamental tyrant that rigidly dictates the scheduling that involves the cultivation of the land!

This was unfathomable to our Mr. Bredouille. Every morning of every day he could be seen leaning and supporting his whole weight against a tree, deeply and intensively absorbed in concentration. He appeared to be struggling in a gigantic effort to solve a huge problem. "What must I do today? What is the most urgent?" he muttered to himself, perspiration running profusely from his forehead. It seemed that the fate of the whole universe rested and weighed heavily upon his shoulders!

The situation was disturbing to an adult but to an immature child, it was hilarious! And it was mind bamboozling enough just to see him leaning there lost in thought without further analysis!

There was something else about this man that was indeed remarkable and intriguing. He was not a man of elaborate means, yet he held on to what he did have with a vengeance!

Unfortunately he had been widowed and left with two children early in life. During busy times he employed someone to prepare meals and assume the general household duties.

One year, during thrashing season, my sister accepted this position. The thrashing crew of about twelve men worked from sunup till sundown. When the season was very late, because of inclement weather, these men sometimes worked day and night to salvage the crops. It was quite evident that they needed the most sustaining nourishment. Juliette set about planning substantial meals. Finding the pantry bare, she requisitioned the necessary materials required: meat, vegetables, ingredients for pies, etc. "Well," exclaimed the irate patron, "these men are not kings. They don't need any meat dishes. They can eat vegetables and potatoes. That's good enough for them. And pies are a luxury. Pies are out of the question!!"

My sister, unable to bear the embarrassment and humiliation of serving such a measly fare to a starving crew, took matters in her own hands. She baked some pies and cakes. Without the master's knowledge she killed two geese that majestically pranced about the farmyard.

The consequences? The thrashing crew relished and devoured the sumptuous fare. The master's wrath? Let's hope it remains buried in the past!

Thus, in spite of all his eccentricities, his bizarre notions, and unique personality, this remarkable individual was a fascinating individual; his idiosyncratic behavior singled him out as one that cannot be cast into the depths of oblivion, and he remains forever in my memories.

Beyond Compare

The Labeaute' family lived in a small cottage across the road from the school. The name may not have been characteristic of the parents' appearance. It was certainly typical of the girls in the family, for all three of them were ravishing beauties. Curly red hair, fair complexion, graceful and with impeccable manners! Their sparkling beauty would have dazzled the judges in a contest and left all their competitors in the shadows.

The parents, if not outstanding in appearance, were most unmistakably so in character. Mrs. Labeaute' had the reputation of being an absolute nag, haughty and domineering. On the other hand, Mr. Labeaute' was known as a timid, self-effacing individual, typical of a hen-pecked husband. The patient benevolent husband was said to acquiesce to all his wife's demands.

Humorous incidences occurring in the family clearly depict these character traits in both the parents. One evening, very late in the night, the lights were out, and silence reigned throughout the house. The family had retired for the night. Suddenly Mrs. Labeaute' bolted upright in her bed and screamed!! "Mr. Labeaute, did you take the cat to the barn?" "Sorry, dear, I completely forgot," replied Mr. Labeaute'. "Mr. Labeaute', take the cat to the barn at once," she commanded, "and don't forget to close the barn door so that it won't get out again." "Yes dear," thus saying, Mr. Labeaute' obediently got up, dressed and carried the cat to the barn.

Many such ridiculous scenes were jokingly circulated in the neighbourhood. Mrs. Labeaute' may have been an overbearing and hen-pecking woman, but she may have been compelled to rule with an iron hand out of necessity. As the responsible head of the household she may have been coerced to do so.

Be that as it may, her qualities and gifts more than compensated for whatever negative traits she may have possessed. She was an idealist; she refused to be victimized or to submit to the deprivations of impossible circumstances that the hostile environment imposed.

She had determined that she would rise above all obstacles and provide her family with a living standard comparable to those of a higher status, both economically and culturally. She managed to teach the girls the social graces pertaining to the upper echelon of society only. Their comportment in any social milieu was irreproachable. Such behavior emanated from a home where the decorum was elevated, flawless!!

The three girls came to school immaculately clean, their beautiful red hair in long curls; not one strand out of place.

But it was the exquisite dresses they wore that were so amazing! They were well designed, made from expensive material, and beautiful. When the girls walked into the classroom they looked as if they had just walked out of a fashion show. They stood out among their classmates, who were dressed in worn farm attire, perhaps patched and threadbare. Folks claimed that Mrs. Labeaute' designed and sewed all the girls' clothes. This woman must have been exceedingly gifted. She managed to be a superior teacher, an outstanding seamstress, the manager of the household, and a role model to her girls, besides keeping the little cottage shining clean. Endowed with remarkable gifts, skills and ingenuity, she managed to give her family a standard of living superior beyond belief.

None But The Brave

The Sui Generis family was the most exclusive family in the environment. Everything about them was different!! Mr. Sui Generis was a remarkably gracious, courteous gentleman, and Mrs. Sui Generis was the most gorgeous, enchantingly and beautiful woman in the surrounding area. Indeed her beauty could have eclipsed that of every modern woman (including those in Hollywood). She had big brown eyes that sparkled whenever she spoke. Curly brown hair framed the contour of her fair oval features; accentuated by the becoming wide brimmed hat she always wore. The three girls had inherited the mother's grace and beauty.

The family lived in a remote, hilly terrain, rough and therefore unsuitable for any form of agriculture. They had their own particular means of providing for their subsistence. It appeared that financial matters were not a major concern. What was so remarkable, so exceptional however, was the happiness, the love and peace that reigned in that home. Although visitors were warmly welcomed in their midst, they did not seem to need or crave the social companionship others could provide. They seemed to be sufficient unto themselves.

It is incomprehensible, utterly mind baffling and bewildering that some humans cannot bear excellence in other realms. A source of trouble must be sought and thence stirred to mar and destroy this perfect harmony. They do not rest or find peace until their evil quest has been satisfied. It must be that the rationale behind this is "what right have they to be so blissfully happy when I am so miserable". Who knows!!! These busy bodies must have been ecstatic because they managed to cook up a scandal involving the male parent. That vicious slander nearly destroyed what was cherished the most; the faith and loyalty to one another, the security in their love, hence all that held the family together so joyfully.

The matter was dragged into court; every effort was made to smear and defame the reputation of the father. As it was later established, the culpable treacherous scheme was that an innocent man be held accountable for the horrendous crime he himself (the perpetrator) had committed. The loyalty and the support of friends and loved ones never faltered. Therefore, in spite of the grievous pain and suffering it had engendered, the slander did not destroy the beautiful relationship that bonded the household together.

The drama of these people's lives did not end there, however. For once destiny has unearthed its prey, the raging fury of its waves will forever lurch (rock) the victim's fate to and fro. A whirlpool of turmoil, churning angrily, follows on the heels of that which preceded it, just as the ebb and rising tide of the waters flow eternally on its way to the sea.

Once the repercussion of the tragedy had somewhat subsided, the family, with the support of their friends, made an effort to resume the normal pattern of their lives. It was not to be.

In her teens, one of the three girls fell madly in love with a boy in the neighborhood, the son of the local tyrant Mr. LeRoi? For reasons yet unknown, the father disapproved of the relationship. It may have been an aftermath of the previous tragedy. This man was not to be trifled with. Like the ancient emperor, he was the <u>law</u>. Or so he claimed! That was before he met this girl. If she was to be denied, she wanted to know the reason for the denial. So she mounted her horse, rode to the boy's house and confronted the startled father, whose word had never been questioned, let alone by a mere slip of a girl. He was totally unprepared for the courage and bold spirit of this girl. The confrontation that ensued was catastrophic. Both were shouting and screaming abuses at each other. She did not back down. She fought fire with fire. It is unknown who got the best of this dreadful open conflict. The poor girl, almost hysterical, rode to our house afterwards. All the family sympathized with her, as we knew the cantankerous man she had had to contend with. Not many months afterwards, the boy married. The poor girl was broken hearted and mourned her loss for many years afterwards. Little did she know how lucky she was, as the son was an exact replica of his tyrannical parent.

Some time afterwards, these remarkable, intrepid people embarked on a venture that again set them in a class of their own; distinguished them from others forever. They decided to travel west in a horse drawn vehicle; a wagon, no less! It must have been a stupendous decision – considering the distance to be covered and the limited distance they would be able to travel in one day. They had procured themselves with camping equipment, groceries, medical supplies and all the necessities essential for such a momentous journey. They did reach their destiny. Months afterwards Juliette's friend (the youngest of the family) wrote from Vancouver. She described, in detail, the exciting and extraordinary experiences the family had met along the way. Apparently they had had no major misfortunes and had enjoyed every single minute of the adventure. Truly only the most gregarious, those with exceptional and boundless courage would undertake such a venture – "None but the brave".

A Contemporary Good Samaritan

There is a spiritual song in the hymnbook at church that contains these lines and I quote "Here I am Lord. I have heard you calling in the night. I will go Lord if you need me. I will hold your people in my heart". It was by these words that a neighbor, a very dear friend, Good Sam, lived. Samuel Labonté, which translates into Sam Good. However as he was the embodiment of "good" I shall call him "Good Sam".

This man must have been in constant dialogue with the Almighty. His life was an exact embodiment of these words. In an effort to picture him precisely and accurately, as he really and truly was, the word "THERE" constantly surfaced in my thoughts. In fact it was the first concept that occurred to me. He was there in times of need, he was there in an emergency, he was there in a crisis. He was always there; ready to render assistance in a crucial situation. His memory conjures an influx of terms that would all very adequately describe him. Compassionate, charitable, kind, accessible, accommodating, etc…yet the most precise is the word "there". Not only was he there for his friends but like the Good Samaritan in the Bible he was there for anyone in times of distress.

A few incidences which emphasizes this man's character follow:

In the dead of winter, on a bitterly cold evening, a young woman carrying two very small children, knocked at his door. She had walked several miles in that brutal weather and almost collapsed with exhaustion. She was half frozen and so were the two children. The older child, a little girl, seemed in good health in spite of having been exposed to the cold, she soon recuperated in the cozy warmth of the house. The baby boy was desperately ill. The poor woman had been begging her husband to take the child to the doctor and had been ignored. The children were starved; there had been little food in the house, and no milk for the baby. In desperation and fearing for the life of her child, the mother ventured to get help. This friend of the family, Good Sam, was the closest and the only possible means of succor. After he and his wife had provided emergency assistance – food, warmth and milk for the baby, our friend took or drove the woman to her sister's home, whereupon the baby was duly taken to a doctor. Given proper nourishment and care the baby survived and was soon in good health.

There was also the episode that involved the diabetic. When Juliette (my sister) arrived at his house, Good Sam immediately saw the terror, the hysteria, in her eyes. He reacted at once. They both practically flew back to the scene where the man had been found. Good Sam alerted the farmer, who at once assumed the responsibility the situation demanded, and drove the frightened girl to her parents' home. To him that was the only thing to do.

There were countless other emergency episodes or incidences in which our "Good Samaritan" performed acts of mercy. These are too numerous to recall or relate.

Besides being the providential "Good Samaritan" this good man was the local dentist. And, ho, how he loathed that self-imposed duty in the relief of suffering. But as much as he despised removing the offending tooth, it was even more painful for him to witness the agony of the patient. So, with his crude surgical medical instruments he would manage to persuade himself reluctantly to do the deed.

A distraught parent brought her young daughter to him one day. The unfortunate child was suffering from an excruciating toothache. It would have been difficult to judge which one was suffering the most, the child or the dentist, as he anticipated the horrible agony the child would endure in the process. "Oh no!" he thought ruefully, "not a child. I cannot do this!" "Could you not take the poor child to a reliable competent dentist?" he asked the parent. "A dentist with proper sedatives to ease the pain and equipped with the proper instruments?" "The nearest dentist is fifteen miles away, and he may not be home!" pleaded the mother. "Besides, even if he were at his office, it would take hours to get there. Do you realize the torment this child would endure before we got there?" The dejected look on the poor man's face was sad to behold. Yet the child's tears and the mother's entreaties prevailed.

Apparently soon after the tooth was removed the pain subsided. Everyone, especially the kind would-be dentist, breathed a sigh of relief and thankfulness.

It is entirely inexplicable how some are showered with innumerable endowments while yet others are visibly deprived of any that are apparent. Or their gifts are hidden and beyond our limited human understanding and intelligence.

So it was that besides being a one man rescuing patrol, a compassionate dentist, a veritable providential angel, this friend was also a musician. He played the violin by ear, but his ear for music was true. He could not tolerate dissonance. He played for his friends, for dances, concerts, in the Church choir and mostly for the pure joy of playing.

How delightful were the evenings when he came to our house with his violin. It always culminated in a concert, a veritable musical extravaganza! Someone accompanying him either on the organ or the guitar and others trying to harmonize either on the violin or on the accordion.

As much as we loved that tall, stalwart, young man, it would have been unthinkable to judge which one we loved more, him or his wife. Together, the couple looked like Mutt and Jeff. For he was so tall, so powerfully built, and she so "petite", so "delicate". Nonetheless, her beauty, her charm, more than compensated whatever she lacked in stature. The charisma, the sweetness of her personality endeared her to all. One evening, after spending an enjoyable social get together; as she prepared to leave our house, she was adjusting a neat little beret on her comely, silky hair. This beret was unusually becoming. It appeared to have been especially designed for her (it was, as either she or my mother had crocheted it). Her appearance, wearing that cute beret, was so remarkable that even my dad remarked on it, "I think she knows how strikingly attractive she looks in that beret," he said. Everyone was stunned. A compliment coming from my dad was a miracle! But for once everyone agreed with him. I believe it was on that same fateful evening that my dad performed another miracle. A double whammy! As she was wrapping her son in warm winter blankets she told my parents how her brother had been diagnosed as a potential tuberculosis victim. He had just been admitted to the sanitarium for further testing. In spite of my mother's reassurance and sympathy she sobbed uncontrollably. "I know that when a patient is admitted to that institution, it is the end," she mourned. "He will never come out again," she continued as she wrapped the baby snugly in his cozy blankets. "My poor brother has been repeatedly accused of being a lazy, worthless fellow. He is branded as having no pride because he cannot support himself. Yet he is too ill to work! How erroneous, brutal and merciless are the judgments of blind ignorance," she resumed through her tears. It was then, after the couple left that my father again complimented our friend. "That little woman is a warm, compassionate human being," he muttered. "She is deeply grieved by her brother's illness. I am truly sorry for her." Her predictions were soon to be realized. Not many months afterwards her brother died.

The happiness (joy), the warmth, this young couple's friendship brought to the family was inexhaustible. The compatibility of interests, aspirations, views and moral standards, involved these two families in practically all the social aspects of their lives.

There was the sharing of meals. Of course in the community where we lived anyone happening to come at mealtime on business or for any reason impromptu always shared whatever food happened to be on the table. But this was different! It was more ceremonious, more festive. It was usually done on special occasions. The menu was elaborate and the food was prepared with care. The guests were formerly invited. The sharing of special meals back and forth on festive occasions occurred several times throughout the year. Sometimes it did not have to be for any specific reason; it was just an excuse to be together and enjoy good company.

Some evenings were spent playing cards. Some in telling stories of the past and many times of mysterious events. Sometimes plain conversation about current topics captured the interest of everyone and was the entertainment for the whole evening. Music, however, was the most frequent limelight and the focus of most evenings. Musical concerts where everyone joined in, musically gifted or not, playing a multitude of instruments. Violins, guitars, an organ, an accordion, a ukulele, mouth organ, xylophone, all synchronized to burst into rapturous, melodious harmony. Each secret longing was "Let this joyful rejoicing be everlasting".

In beautiful sunny summer weather, these folks shared a picnic spot on the fine sandy beaches of "Devil's Lake", renowned for its beauty and glorious sand. Not only our folks, but the whole community gathered on the beaches after the Sunday church celebration. Friends gathered together, spread blankets to sit on the sand, set their lunches on a tablecloth and shared the food they had brought. It was a time of recreation and socialization. The children enjoyed the swimming and boating, while most of the adults were content to visit and relax.

Kindred Spirits?

Sometimes I wonder what motive lay at the root of this indestructible relationship. A bond so solid that it remained constant and persisted even after the death of my parents. A bond that emanated into something even greater than friendship. In later years the couple became one of us (our brother, our sister) or (brothers and sisters all).

Sometimes I think that it was their mutual passion for music, a passion that eclipsed everything else in their lives. This obsession manifested itself conspicuously, unmistakably in both households. At the time money was out of the question. Our friend traded a cow for his first violin – a violin that he wanted above everything else. My mother, on the other hand, managed to purchase an organ. She also managed to fill with musical instruments a house that was equipped with the barest of necessities. It is quite evident therefore that music was a priority in both households.

This relationship may have been motivated by a strong adherence to a common ideology, a strong sense of justice and a deep compassion for the suffering of others.

But transcending all these was the compulsion to assist and support those in need, be it financial, physical, or emotional. This compulsion was the origin of what evolved in a wonderful friendship as related in the following paragraphs.

Previous to their union, the couple's marriage status was beset by many obstacles. Although their affection for each other was sincere, other parties interfered and were responsible for much pain and heartache. Our hero's mother was violently opposed to the marriage and strongly disapproved of her son's fiancé. This imperious lady's authority over her domain was absolute and uncontested. No one dared to cross her domineering rule. Not even her husband! Her whole household cringed under her command. It is obvious that when she disapproved of her son's choice of mate all hell broke loose. The son, torn between his mother's fury and his love for his fiancé, was driven reluctantly to the altar. This should have been followed by happiness and celebrations. However it was not to be. The bride was forced to live with her mother-in-law who treated her with contempt. This woman used every possible excuse to demean her son's spouse and to wound her feelings grievously. During that period the pain she suffered inflicted by her mother-in-law's cruelty was compensated by the love for her beloved husband.

Eventually the couple was able to establish a home of their own. Their life was thereafter filled with love and happiness.

Undeterred, the mother-in-law tried persistently to impose her iron authority on their lives. These unwelcomed interferences caused many problems and sorrow. But it was this lady's tenacious resolve to discredit her daughter-in-law in the eyes of the community and friends which was most disastrous. In spite of this conflict, the couple's love surmounted and survived these assaults.

In Defense (Debatable!)

It is not only unfair but also one-sided, disproportionate to think that this mother-in-law (our friend's) was evil. On the contrary she led an exemplary life. That is exactly what the problem was. People who walk the straight and narrow, never stepping an inch off the beaten path, cannot bear failure in another. They are so virtuous themselves that they are unable to visualize any other way. Any divergence is for them as excruciatingly painful as dissonance is to a fanatic musician. They judge others by the same standards as they judge themselves. Many times that judgment is based on what seems apparent or heresy: not on truth. Truth is not evident; neither are the circumstances. Therefore they are not taken into consideration or ignored completely. Instead of asking themselves "What would I have done in a similar circumstance?" or "What lies beyond this situation?" they simply ask "How could they have committed such an evil deed?"

There is another consideration in defense of this well-intentioned woman. Parents tend to be biased or hopelessly blind in matters concerning their children. They want to give them the world on a silver platter, nothing else but the best. Is it any wonder that they (insist on and) are so discriminating when choosing a lifetime partner for their loved ones. Is it any wonder that would-be mates for their dear ones are under such stringent scrutiny? Although the choice is not theirs to make many parents cannot detach themselves and interfere. Their children's happiness is an obsession.

Parents should not be condemned for this; it is simply human nature, a desire to protect their own. It is indeed a great sacrifice for some parents to allow their children to lead their own lives.

It was then during these troubled times when everyone else was ready to judge and condemn that my mother took the couple under her protective wings, supporting them, ready to defend them with vengeance, against anyone who dared to attack or harm her protégés in any form. It goes without saying that no one ever had the audacity to do so openly when my mother was present. That support in times of distress was what endeared my mother to this grateful couple. It was more than anything else the seed that flourished into such a binding friendship.

Wisdom Galore

Another member of the community who stands out among the multitudes in my souvenirs was an absolute genius, Mr. Solomon. Although he excelled in many other fields, architecture was his specialty. He designed and built two splendid homes for a fastidious local resident. The first was well designed, structurally sound and comfortable. The second was a masterpiece, a veritable castle! The whole neighbourhood marveled at this spectacular achievement. Unfortunately it was situated on a low mountainous ridge, a rocky terrain unsuitable for cultivation, and had to be abandoned.

Because of his great intellectual capacity, this man was well informed. He could speak intelligently on any field; politics, current events, social concerns and issues, art… He was a most interesting conversationalist. Regrettably the couple had only one living daughter. Many children had been born to them but tragically died in infancy from some unknown children's disease. The grateful parents doted on this one surviving child.

It is said that a carpenter's home is the most dilapidated of the neighbourhood. Indeed this saying applied in every respect to this most brilliant architect in our "neighborhood". Living in a mansion was not his priority. It did little to improve the sorry condition of the family home. It did not seem to be that important to his wife or daughter either. All three of them, the carpenter, his wife and daughter, seemed to be blissfully content just to be together.

This ingenious man had constructed, unaided, a miniature factory for his daughter in the basement of their house. It consisted of an immense loom, stretching wall to wall and reaching as far up as the ceiling. There was a hand made spinning wheel, carders, a reel, and all the tools necessary to spin wool into yarn and thence to weave it into woolen cloth. The whole apparatus was magnificent!

His daughter must have also been creative as an artisan. She wove woolen fabrics and blankets in which she created artistic designs.

A Rescue

Solomon was accredited for having saved the life of a drowning friend and neighbor. The two men were enjoying an afternoon swim when his friend was seized with cramps. Of course Mr. Solomon swam to his aid. Unfortunately the drowning man would not allow anyone to pull him to shore. He struggled violently. "He almost drowned us both," the exhausted rescuer lamented. "He ferociously fought every effort I made to save him. It took every ounce of my strength to restrain him and drag him to shore. For some frantic moment I feared he would pull us both under." Later the gratitude of his friend was enormous, of course!!

Justice! For Whom?

It is with great misgivings and hesitation that I even dare to relate one regrettable and painful episode that occurred in the vicinity. It is deplorably tainted with the wiles and schemes of power and politics. Power that makes lambs into wolves, and politics that makes justice a financial issue. These, along with any other controversial issue, are taboo in the upper echelon of our society. Constrained by the fangs of power the media is coerced in spreading only politically acceptable propaganda and prohibited in voicing any contentious, critical or sensitive issues. Thus political intrigue and charm using the strong influence of the media sways the masses to conform and comply with their every whim. Complimenting and advantageous to their cause, ordinary people tend to seek the status quo in which they hope to find happiness and beauty. They tend to shun or steer clear of any unpleasantness or of any factor that may cause them pain. For that attitude they are irreproachable. The exigencies of survival are harrowing, stressful enough for those who have been unable to experience the rapture embodied in the gift of life itself. They cannot be penalized. Shouldering additional burdens would lead them to despair.

Yet, is it possible to condone the fact that most bury their heads in the sand when something painful is in the wind, whenever a

formidable problem looms ahead. Thus hoping that if they bury it deep
enough the problem will go away; that the hurt will dissolve! At times
peeking to see if the storm has subsided and emerging only when the
weather is fair, when the hurricane has blown itself away at last!

For None But The Mighty

The unfortunate incidence originated with a dispute involving
young adults from two neighborhood families. Two youths verbally
assaulted a member of a nearby family, using foul, vulgar, abusive
language. Traumatized and utterly devastated the victim sought the
support of her family.

Overwhelmed with shock the family made a concerted effort to
comprehend what motive had instigated this vicious attack. At last the
matter was brought to court.

The youth's family retained the most reputable, prominent
lawyer in the state. He was reputed as being able to acquit his clients of
their crimes irrespective of the gravity, even murder! The victim's family
could not afford a lawyer... Thus the malfeasant were, of course,
acquitted. The eloquent lawyer insinuated that the defendants were as
innocent as newborn lambs and that the victim was the true culprit. It is
incredible that this lawyer, without a grain of integrity, later became a
prominent political leader.

The fact that this capable lawyer was instrumental in the youth's
acquittal was to be expected, and was probably accepted by the victim's
family. It has always been a well-known assumption that money talks
and that it has always been the supreme power.

But what was so incomprehensible, so mystifying, utterly
disconcerting, was the fact that, leaving a house full of children, the
victim's mother was incarcerates to defray the cost of the whole affair.
Thus the innocent were punished and paid the price for the culpable'
transgressions, and that because the innocent lacked the almighty dollar.

Philosophers claim that history has a tendency to repeat itself.
And so in this story there was almost an identical repetition of the first
episode. The same families were involved and the same type of
transgression. Only the offenders were much younger and the victims
extremely timid with a remarkably different temperament. It was some
years later and to all outward appearances the feud between the two
families had somewhat subsided. A truce of some sort had been called

and the families were on speaking terms. It seemed perfectly logical that a mutual trust between them had been reestablished. This was crucial as the children from these two families attended the same rural school. Subsequently, unaware of the peril, two young girls from the previously injured family accepted a ride with the boys from the other family. The girls were unsuspicious, as these boys were their classmates.

No sooner were they on their way that the violent, verbal abuse erupted. Heinous, obscene language spurted out of these boys' foul mouths. The attack was so unexpected, so vicious, and unwarranted that it was beyond all justification.

There are certain deep emotional crises that harbor in the abyss of the soul and which are so painful, so hideous, that they are buried profoundly hidden in the depths of the heart. They are the secrets that are unspeakable, too horrid to be disclosed. Secrets that shatter the heart with anguish. It was years afterwards that this unfortunate girl related the incidence to a trusted friend. "I could not understand why he was speaking to us that way," she sobbed, he spoke words that were so vile, so heinous, so obscene, that it was as if the venom from Medusa serpents was gushing out of his filthy mouth. I should have jumped out, but I froze, paralyzed with disgust and repugnance. I was scandalized by words that I had never heard before, feeling so humiliated, violated, dirty, that to hide in a dark closet forever was my sole reaction. In the future I will avoid these boys like poison, even if I have to walk miles to do so."

The poor girl could not understand why these boys abused her and her sister. Why, indeed!

The only logical conclusion. They must have remembered that under similar circumstances the law acquitted such despicable, contemptible, loathsome and infamous behavior. They must have felt that for them nothing is beyond limits. The power that their father's money had given them was boundless. "Carte blanche!"

Meditating over these episodes, I am still tormented, trying in vain to unravel the rationale and justice behind all these proceedings. And I ask myself "What is sine qua non (indispensable); justice, or the power that money buys?" It appears that money and power are one and the same tyrant; a tyrant with a dual personality! Money dictates, while power administers and enforces. Together they are omnipotent. Like Emil Zola's monstrous human devouring machine, their capacious far-reaching, wide-open jawed tentacles grasp, engulf, and crunch all unsuspecting penniless human targets. For the unfortunate, the poor, there is no refuge from the talons of oppression. They are the clay molded and exploited at the hands of power, the potter.

THE NATIVES

We lived in a community where a great percentage of the population was of native origin. Most had accepted and become assimilated to the white man's way of life. They were, much like their neighbors, farmers. They were commendable citizens, honorable and law abiding. They were also extremely religious and had irreproachable moral values.

The natives who lived on the reserves were different. They could not understand or accept our way of life! Therefore they continued to live according to their customary and traditional culture. To these proud people acculturation was a process that was oppressive, demeaning and therefore unacceptable. They felt that those subjected to this process were stripped of their dignity and the essence of their individuality. They felt that it robbed them of their language, their religion, and of their means of providing for their own needs – that their title, their rights as a proud, unique and distinct people had been ravaged.

The most devastating crime committed against these people was to strip them of their human dignity, to destroy their self-esteem and make them feel worthless, shiftless rabble.

Granted that their means of providing for their needs severely conflicted with that of the white population. It is quite evident that farmers and hunters cannot coexist in the same territory. One activity is entirely adverse to the other.

Therefore as hunting as a means of subsistence was no longer feasible, these people should have been strongly encouraged and urged to provide for their <u>own</u> needs in the same manner as everyone else. They should have been given the same opportunity on an equal basis and terms while retaining their own identity. This would evidently have required tremendous efforts: teaching, patience, tolerance, and compassion. But it would have averted the formidable problem that Canadians encountered in the future and that has never been resolved because of its complexity. As an emergency measure, they were herded unto reserves much like inhuman creatures. A mere subsistence allowance was grudgingly doled out to them. This rash, thoughtless action compounded the gravity of the situation and had astronomical ramifications. It was the materialization of a colossal statement. It blatantly stated that these people were inferior, incompetent, worthless, and therefore unable to care for themselves. This statement was persistently inculcated in all relationships with them. Consequently the spirit of these proud people was crushed within them, only the shell of who they were remained!

Was it any wonder that at the mercy of conquering power these people felt defeated. Not only did they feel that defeat in the power of the assailant, but they felt it in their very souls. So they wallowed in despair and hopelessness. Many natives on the reserves had given up hope. They were unable to visualize any course of action that might improve their situation. To these the only alternative was to assuage the pain of subordination and degradation. Hence many turned to alcohol and drugs to alleviate the suffering and humiliation. It seems that many had accepted and continue to live in deplorable, impoverished circumstances.

Numerous members of the community were appalled and greatly distressed by the misery that plagued these people. The suffering they endured, the abuse, the injustices, and contempt inflicted upon them by their white brothers was horrendous.

Some unscrupulous shopkeepers charged those unsuspecting victims double or triple the amount they ordinarily demanded from other customers for the same value. Unless someone intervened on their behalf, they were forced to pay these outrageous prices. Others who knew the natives' vulnerability for liquor sold them extract (vanilla, etc…) in guise of alcohol. This was often purchased with treaty money; the money that was intended for food and their basic needs. As a consequence of these despicable criminal proceedings the children were deprived of nourishment and of the barest essentials for survival. While the parents caroused in a drunken orgy, the unfortunate children screamed, starving, scantily clad, shivering barefooted in the snow.

Bearing witness to such an incidence, one wonders if all humans belong to the same species. Or is it that the hearts of some are fabricated of love and others of pure stone.

Our home was often a refuge for these people. It provided a haven where warmth and a cup of tea was always available. The farm was situated midway between two native reserves. There was a continual coming and going from one of these reserves to the other and vice versa. This constant transit was presumably to visit friends or relatives. It was impossible to verify their motives as most of these natives spoke very little English. During the summer this trek presented little hardship, except perhaps fatigue. However, during the severe winter temperatures, sometimes dipping down to 60 degrees below zero Celsius, it was another matter. Travel in a horse drawn sleigh, lacking the warmth of modern well-insulated winter clothing was, to say the least, hazardous! This of course was immaterial, as these people did not possess the necessary funds to purchase whatever clothes were available. Whenever they reached our house, they were frozen (like icicles), hungry and exhausted. They always stopped. Their horses were fed. They were allowed to sit by the fire until they were warm and comfortable. A cup of tea and whatever food was available was provided. This hospitality was exceedingly appreciated, as a cup of tea to the natives is as sacred as it is to the English. The refuge from the bitter cold, the nourishment provided them with renewed vigor to proceed on their journey. Is it any wonder that they beheld my mother as a providential angel? As these stopovers were regular occurrences, they were accepted as normal and most have left no lasting impressions.

I have, however, horrid nightmares and am constantly haunted by the memory of one of those incidences. On a bitterly cold day, a family of natives had, as usual, stopped at our house to warm up. However, there were two in the group whose image keeps recurring as a phantom in my mind and cannot be erased. The blind grandfather, white haired, thin, wrinkled, was the very symbol of suffering and destitution. He was scantily clad and shivering from the cold. He endured his plight patiently without a trace of self-pity. He seemed to accept his fate as a given matter. He spoke little English and was trying to tell my dad how old he was. Effectively, he flashed the fingers on both hands six times then three more fingers to show he was sixty-three.

The other disturbing and persistent image is of a fifteen or sixteen year old boy. He was tall, very slight, and quite handsome. He was wearing a brand new denim coverall. He must not have been wearing underwear underneath those. He wore no jacket. He was frozen! Although he was seated closest to the fire, he couldn't seem to get warm. He did not merely shiver, he vibrated with cold. His predicament was most lamentable. I am still vibrating in my heart with him and praying that they (his friends) allowed him time to get warm before resuming their journey.

There is another incidence that haunts my childhood memories. It is the picture of a native girl kneeling behind the cloakroom door at our country school, cringing with despair and weeping uncontrollably. The image of that poor, miserable child hiding there still torments me, as it flashes before me as clearly and distinctly as if she was kneeling there yet, right before my eyes. "What on earth are you doing there?" I asked seeing her there. "I am praying," was the pathetic answer. "I am asking God to make them stop persecuting me."

"Where was the teacher?" I asked myself overwhelmed with confusion and chagrin. Was she or he unaware that this persecution was going on? Or are children more perceptive and sensitive than adults to human suffering? Or do they simply turn away, unable to bear the pain of it all? The mind of a child is unable to fully comprehend the complexity of such a grave occurrence. It can only surmise that the abuse must be stopped. Immaturity inhibits considerations of the intricacies involved in the solution of a difficult problem. This problem had been accumulating over a long period of time and was no doubt rooted in prejudice or discrimination.

Most of the students attending the little country school in the district were from French Canadian families. One boy however was from English parents and three were from a Metis family. The two Metis boys were well behaved and were well adapted to the school situation. The girl was developmentally challenged. She was also well behaved and in any other circumstance would never have caused any problems. Unfortunately, four of the students were victims of parental abuse. As is often the case, these children followed in the abusive parents (footsteps) example. Because of her problem the Metis girl made a vulnerable target. Consequently, the abusive boys harassed her continually. They tormented her in the schoolyard, during recess, on the way home from school. They never stopped. Although the abuse was not physical, the venom that poured from these boys' malicious tongues was hideous. And of course that poor defenseless girl was always at the butt of these cruel, beastly attacks. Hence unable to bear the ferocity of the assault one day she hid behind the cloakroom door.

Looking back, it is almost incredible that this unfortunate girl did not complain to her parents, or that her two brothers remained silent. None of the other students were. They were outraged and could not understand why no one came to aid this innocent victim. It is incomprehensible that they did not. But they never failed to intervene on her behalf or to render detailed accounts of the incidence to their own parents. Therefore all the parents, except the girl and the abusers', were aware of the situation.

On the way home from school one day the persecution was unbearable. The girl lost her temper and with her lunch kit as a weapon she hurled a gigantic blow to the tormenter's 'head. He suffered a severe cut to his forehead. The reaction was immediate and overwhelming. A board meeting was instantly summoned.

Most truly civilized human beings have abhorrence for abuse. The word itself is repugnant. It denies and destroys the rights and freedom of the individual. This belief must have been firmly ingrained in my mother's psyche because a bully to her was intolerable. Anyone using his superiority in any way to take advantage of anyone weaker than themselves or to demean them was to her despicable. Like a knight in shining armor she rose to the defense of the oppressed. Being well informed she was well prepared to give evidence of what had transpired on the day in question.

A general meeting had been called; the trustees and parents included. It was felt that the issue concerned members of the school district as a whole.

The plaintiff, the tormentor's father, rose, indignant! "This is an outrage," he thundered. "My child was viciously attacked and severely wounded by a student on the way home from school. This student," he continued, "is a menace to the safety of our children. I demand, nay, I insist that she be expelled immediately, never to be readmitted in our school," he roared imperiously.

Fortunately the members of the school board (my mother being one of them) had been alerted concerning the events that had preceded and caused this occurrence. This man's loud threats and booming accusations usually intimidated everyone present at every meeting. My mother rose and confronted the plaintiff: "Do you know, sir," she demanded, "who the real victim is in this case?" For a moment the gentleman remained silent, confused, as he prepared to resume his tirade. Previously no one had ever dared to challenge his crushing attacks. He was at the moment preparing to resume his assault full force. He had not anticipated the wisdom and the factual knowledge of the incidences his opponents possessed.

"Sir," repeated my mother 'undaunted', "are you aware that your son is not the victim, but the assailant in this case?"

There was another moment of silence as he stared at my mother. Disregarding her comments he again prepared to assert his grievances and demand justice. Again he was interrupted by a wave of the hand and a calm confident voice. "Sir," she said, "if you would kindly sit down and stop bellowing, perhaps the committee can get down to the truth of this matter after all the evidence has been presented." The gentleman dismissed this last statement much as he would shoo the aggravations of a buzzing fly. "There is only one truth," retorted he, "the only evidence we need is clearly the gash on my son's forehead," but he sat down.

Then in a calm, affirmative tone my mother began the recital of the incidences when his children, one boy especially, had harassed, tormented, and abused not only the unfortunate girl, but her whole family because they were different. The persecutions, the insults were constant. The brothers simply ignored the name calling and dirt slung at them. The girl, however, was unable to ignore the abuses as they were mostly directed at her. She could not pretend indifference or distance herself from her tormentors because of limited space.

On and on the episodes were presented, including the girl's intercession to heaven, since no one on earth bothered to help her or cared.

The other board members also related what their children had witnessed. As usual when one speaker has the courage to stand up for justice all others follow suit. All members present corroborated the grievances the Metis family had endured at the hands of the supposedly victimized plaintiff's sons. The meeting must have adjourned as it does in a real courtroom with "Case dismissed" ruling.

Did the insults and the persecution cease hereafter? That important fact has vanished from my memory; regrettably!

There was another episode involving a Metis family. In a large city, teaching grade one in a transient district can be quite interesting and can conjure up some momentous experiences. On one occasion a brother and his sister complained almost every day that their classmates would gang up on them on the way home and beat them. The mother alerted the school principal and the teacher concerned. No amount of chastising, threatening, or moralizing proved effective. So the principal requested that the victims' mother come to the school, hoping that together they might be able to find a solution to the problem.

The usual conversation ensued. The reasons why the children were assaulted or beaten were explored. The mother suggested that it was because they were Metis. Both of the children were very timid and would not have challenged or provoked their classmates to fight. At last, after many suggestions had been presented the principal astonished the poor mother by saying, "Tell your children that sometimes the only way to treat a bully is by giving him a dose of his own medicine. Why don't you get a group of your friends to show these bullies how it feels to be beaten for no reason." "Well," said the wise mother, "violence breeds more violence! The attacks would continue to accelerate and compound the problem. When these troublemakers are aware that my children do not defend themselves, they will get bored and desist."

She was right! The problem gradually solved itself.

The wisdom of this mother's words was like a bombshell. "Who was the teacher that day?" the teacher asked herself.

It is indeed unfortunate that this wise mother cannot share her philosophy with the leaders of world nations. It would undoubtedly restore peace among nations, the people of the world.

Although the family's contact with our many native neighbors was at times to render assistance and support, most of the relationships were positive and pleasurable. Most, at least in the immediate neighbourhood, are endowed with remarkable artistic talents. These talents are especially manifested in music and rhythm. This gift is expressed in the performance of their "Pow-Wow".

In our neighborhood many were skilled violinists. Two of our friends, although they had had no training in musical theory, were experts. Their performances were so exquisite that they could have competed in any of the annual violin festivals held across Canada. Unfortunately these two boys volunteered as privates during the World War II and never returned. Their loss left an empty space in the hearts of all those who had known them.

Native performers usually played the music for the local weekly dances at "Camp Lake" as the makeshift hall was called. The chief, Mr. Richard, was a fun loving native man who possessed such a charming personality that everyone was attracted to him. He organized and directed these weekly fun events. He called the quadrilles and announced the numbers that would follow. Everyone looked forward to these weekly events, including all the young members of our family.

There were also hilarious incidences when the natives stopped at the house on their frequent journey to visit their friends and relatives. The absurdity of these episodes rendered them quite bizarre.

On one occasion, the family evidently must have been lacking butter for some time. There must also have been a problem in getting some, to the great displeasure of the younger members of the family. At any rate a family of natives happened to drive by the house. It must have been summer because they didn't stop for tea or to warm up. As they went by (the road was right in front of the house) one of the boys shouted "Stop them! Stop them! Ask them if they will trade the baby for butter!"

Another family yarn was that these transient people planned to kidnap the baby one day. They were fascinated by the baby's fair complexion and blue eyes. Whether or not there had been any threats or some indication of this abduction was unclear. It was taken seriously enough however to warrant the continual vigilant surveillance by the adults in the family.

Natives are remarkably talented and skilled in the fabrication of unique and exquisite crafts. Our house was always full of native crafts traded for money, food, or anything they needed. There were numerous baskets, hand woven from the tender branches of the willow tree and used as sewing boxes. There were jackets and moccasins made from deer hides and exquisitely decorated with beadwork designs. The sale of these crafts helped the natives in their difficult struggle to survive in a culture that was, and still is, foreign to some of them.

All the members of our family respected and valued our native neighbors. All endeavored to champion, uphold and plead their cause.

STRANGER THAN FICTION

The Lure of "Power"

While working south of the border, my father had the opportunity of visiting and attending many world famous attractions. One of the most spectacular was the Barnum and Bailey Circus, known as "The Greatest Show on Earth". The circus was at the height of its fame. Its spectacles were so unique and varied, it delighted its audiences. My father never wearied of describing the unique features and acts included in the show. Some of these featured exceptional human beings like Charles Stratton, the famous "General Tom Thumb", a dwarf who always appeared with his wife (also a dwarf). Another incredible peculiarity was "Joyce Heth" who was supposedly 160 years old and claimed to have been George Washington's nurse. There were also some famous animals like "Jumbo", the white elephant and a live hippopotamus. What strangely amazed my father was a horse that could add and subtract by using its hooves. When he was asked if the answer was correct he would nod his head "yes" if it was right and shake it "no" when he had arrived at the wrong answer. There were countless incredulous attractions that held the audience mesmerized. Having been fortunate enough to attend such a spectacular world famous attraction was indeed an once-in-a-lifetime experience. Its many features and spectacles had even delighted Queen Victoria when the circus toured Europe from 1840 to 1865. The queen was fascinated by the antics of the amazing "General Tom Thumb" with whom she was photographed on one occasion.

To my father, however, there was one attraction that was the spotlight of the whole circus, the most amazing, and the highlight that transcended all others. It featured the exploits and contests of physical power and endurance. Those tests and competitions of strength held the audience spellbound with wonder. It is true that physical prowess has been admired from the beginning of times. The memory of those endowed with its extraordinary gift was (and is) held with pride. It was especially so at the beginning of the 19th century in Eastern Canada and the States. This was irrefutably corroborated in my father's tales of valor.

Consequently the Barnum Bailey and other circuses were not unique in featuring this form of entertainment. It attracted such admiration and its popularity was so intense that it was a form of recreation anywhere that the male population congregated. Especially in the lumber camps, along with the recital of tall tales, it was an after work form of entertainment. The competitions of strength were dead serious.

Louis Cyr

It was probably in the Barnum Bailey Circus that my dad witnessed the remarkable exploits of many historical celebrities. Among those was the invincible Louis Cyr, who during the later part of the 19th century was renowned to be the strongest man in the world[4]. Born in Quebec he was feted as a national hero, the pride of the Quebecois! His astonishing strength amazed his audiences wherever he performed. A natural showman, he toured the States with his own show on numerous occasions. In 1892 he joined the world famous Ringling Brothers Circus. That is likely where my father witnessed his incredible performances. One of his most outstanding feats was lifting a 230-pound barbell with one hand.

Legends claim that he was a fun loving, outgoing individual. He loved dancing and playing the violin. He delighted in holding his audiences spellbound, breathless as they witnessed the exhibitions of his incredulous strength.

Louis Cyr was recognized as the world champion in weight lifting when he established his record of 273 pounds in London. This outstanding feat had never been challenged until it was surpassed by Victor De Lamarre. De Lamarre repeatedly demonstrated in his performances his incredible record of 309½ pounds, by raising the barbell shoulder high and extending its weight at arms length. The performances in which this 19th century Hercules exhibited his formidable strength held his audiences enthralled.

Perhaps the most outstanding, unbelievable of his exploits was lifting, tied to his back, a 1200 pound horse to the top of a telephone pole. Another, even more astounding, was supporting on his back (on all fours) a platform on which a car loaded with passengers crossed back and forth. According to the book by L' Abbe' De Lamarre[2], no one has or will ever be able to challenge his record. Records claim that he will remain the most powerful man forever.

Many of De Lamarre's performances were witnessed by my father who was overwhelmed by this Samson's strength.

There is a legend circulating in Quebec that De Lamarre's strength was a divine gift.

It happened while he was working in a lumber camp as a "porteur". There was no access road to the camp. Therefore these "porteurs" lugged all the camp's supplies on their backs. The legend goes on to say that one day a lumberman or member of the crew was dangerously ill. Fearing death and being very religious he begged to see a priest. This was an almost impossible request. The camp was miles from the nearest town and there was no suitable means of transportation. The foreman, knowing the complexity of the task, was at a loss. At last he yielded to the sick man's entreaties and sent De Lamarre to fetch the priest. It had stormed for several days and the trail was covered with mud. This, for De Lamarre, who was young and agile, was no problem. The return journey was another matter. It was indeed difficult for the old priest, wearing a long sautane, and who had never walked such a distance to keep up with the young Victor. The story goes on to say that the pair came to a creek that, because of the heavy rains, had overflowed its banks.

"Well," declared the priest, "this is the end of the road. It is entirely impossible for me to cross this creek." "Don't worry, Father," assured Victor, "There is no problem. I'll carry you across." Whereupon Victor put the priest over his shoulder and carried him across the stream.

The priest was astounded. "Young man," he declared, "henceforth, whatever obstacle lies ahead in your path, you will overcome!" Young, with the boundless confidence of youth, Victor was unimpressed by the priest's prediction. He dismissed it as an expression of gratitude. Later, nonetheless, he became aware that he could lift with little effort any burden, regardless of the callosity of its weight. He also noticed that his fellow workers always called upon him when faced with an especially massive encumbrance. As he meditated upon this it appeared strange, weird that they should rely on him, as he was the youngest in the camp.

At last the priest's prophecy came flashing back to him. Gradually he began to test his physical power. His strength never failed him.

At first he used his amazing gift to assist anyone in need. For instance, on one occasion he lifted onto the road a car that was in the ditch, buried hubcap deep in the mud.

He performed many acts of mercy that required extraordinary strength. Later he began to put on performances exhibiting his formidable strength for public entertainment. The legend has it that he believed his strength was a divine gift. He always opened his performances by making the sign of the cross; apparently asking for God's blessing. It also confirmed his deep religious faith.

Victor De Lamarre is celebrated as a French Canadian hero[2]. The village of his birth is named after him. The people in Quebec speak of their hero with great pride.

As previously mentioned, physical strength was greatly esteemed during the 19th century. It was customary for sailors, soldiers and men employed in the lumber industry (lumberjacks as they were called) to gather after work at a public pub or tavern to relax and enjoy a beer. There was usually loud talk, boasting and sometimes heated disputes. These often culminated into competitions, a contest of strength to determine who was the most powerful or the champion among them. On such an occasion the announcer dared anyone in the crowd to challenge the champion of the recent contest. Joe Monteferrand, a tall, robust sixteen year old youth stepped forward, sleeves rolled up ready for combat. In an instant he had his opponent lying face down at his feet.

The news spread rapidly from one tavern to the next and Joe became famous. As his fame spread, Joe decided to test his strength against greater, more famous and renowned opponents. For thirty years he held the title of champion – the strongest man in the region.

Along the Autaouais River there is a bridge that separates Hull from Bytown. Joe's camp was situated on one side of that river. The occupants of the camp across the river were hostile. Joe got wind that a confrontation between the two camps was in the offing. It was rumored that the ensuing skirmishes would be dreadful. Joe stood on the bridge, alone, facing the opposite bank and ready to confront the enemy. It was one against a hundred!! But as each opponent attacked, big Joe forced his retreat, digging his heels in the chin of some and throwing the others in the river. So effective was his one-man stand, that the assailants beat a hasty retreat.

On another occasion, Joe was short of cash. He asked the innkeeper for credit until spring. To show his gratitude he took a somersault and left the imprint of his boot in the ceiling of the tavern!

One hundred years after the death of Joe Monteferrand, Gilles Vigneault wrote a song in praise of this remarkable man[5].

Doubtless there were numerous others endowed with Herculean strength. Louis Cyr, De Lamarre, the Beaupre' giant and Joe Monteferrand lived and performed remarkable exploits during my father's lifetime. He actually witnessed some of the exploits and displays of their formidable power.

A Great Giant

The unprecedented meeting with the giant Beaupre' was another incidence in my father's life that was phenomenal. It was an event that he related with great enthusiasm. It was a monumental episode he had experienced and which he recalled with enormous fervor.

The encounter was purely coincidental. The giant walked into a bar one day where my father was having a beer with some friends. As usual everyone in the bar stared at the giant's phenomenal height. Apparently his head almost touched the ceiling which measured eight feet in height from the floor. His appearance caused a great commotion, absolute pandemonium! Everyone crowded around him, hoping to get a closer look. They hoped to engage him in a conversation, as he was a very famous man. Unfortunately, and because of his stature, he was constantly harassed by brazen, impudent rogues. These miscreants hoped to gain renown and prestige by defeating this remarkable man in single combat. That occasion was no exception. He was challenged by an unruly youth. The giant's response was typical of his genteel, amiable nature. "I am a man of peace," he calmly asserted, "and I refuse to take part in any act of violence or disturbance that would cause trouble of any sort." Thus, discomfited, his tormentor shamefully vanished into the crowd.

It is not certain where my father met this famous giant. Whether it was the giant toured Canada or while he was employed by the Barnum Bailey Circus at St. Louis World's Fair.

The tragedy of his life caused by his unusual size and strength and those who exploited him even after his death is indeed regrettable. The National Film Board of Canada 1987 has complete and authentic records of his career and life history[3]. Born in 1881 in Willow Bunch, Saskatchewan, he died in 1904 and was buried in 1990 when his ashes were returned to his family.

STRANGE WEIRD TALES

Weird

Another tale that is characteristic of the beliefs and general culture of the times is that of "La Jangleuse". Although partially based on facts, it reflects the superstitious beliefs that inspired terror in the people. These beliefs were also instrumental in their behaviour and attitudes. According to Casgrain "La Jangleuse" was the embodiment of Indian imagination and of their legends. She was known as the "Dame aux Glaieuls" by the French and English population, and as the "Matchi Skouiau" or the evil woman by the natives. She was supposed to be invisible during the day. She would appear at midnight. Crowned with gladiolas she had picked in the shrubs that grew along the riverbank she proceeded to make her invocations to the "Great Manitou". Crouched behind the shrubs she would lie in wait for little children. Woo to any of them who fell within her grasp. On one occasion she was held responsible for the torture of a woman, Mrs. Hauel, who was on her way to join her wounded husband. In collaboration with the Iroquois the tales of their evil treachery is endless.

The author, Henri Casgrain[1], does not mention what the inhabitants of the region recount. Their version insists that when she appeared she was being consumed by burning flames. A low chant announced her presence. Sailing down the stream in a canoe manned by Iroquois, she would rise seemingly consumed by crimson, burning flames. Petrified, the enemy fled. They believed that this evil woman had supernatural powers. Needless to say, the Iroquois reined supreme, uncontested in the region.

According to the legend it is little wonder that "La Jangleuse" instilled horror, not only in the hearts of the warriors, but in every man, woman and child who inhabited the shores of the St. Lawrence River.

"This superstitious legend is still believed by many. In fact, they believe that the tracks embedded in the rocks facing the river were imprinted by this mysterious, evil woman."

Alexis, The Invincible

There was also the tale of "Alexis le Trotteur" whose real name was Alexis Lapointe, and whose running speed was unsurpassed or unheard of. He raced in competitions with horses and trains. He was able to run 240 kilometers in one day. His stride was six meters long. Apparently these amazing feats were due to his extraordinary physical build. He was said to be double jointed and have the legs of a horse. He was a sensation in Charlevois, Lac St. Jean, Quebec where he lived. The legend would have it that he'd grab a whip made from a willow branch and whip himself until he had reached his maximum speed. Some say that he whipped himself all the way until he stopped running.

Horror, Unmitigated

In the early settlement of Canada (and of the States) the lumber industry was crucial to the economical needs of the habitant, or settler. The young men made their way and arrived at the lumber camps early in the fall and left late in the spring in order to participate in the cultivation of the soil. The long trek to and from the camp was "on foot" as there were as yet no passable roads for vehicles. Thus some "entrepreneurs" had set up some "inns" or resting points along the way for the weary travelers conveniences. These "inns" indeed provided a lucrative business for the innkeeper, as the men on the return journey from the camp were loaded with all their winter's earnings. It was also a haven for the exhausted men on their journey home.

There is a legend that relates the fate of an unsuspecting, trusting youth on his journey home from the lumber camp. Being extremely tired he begged for food and shelter at one of these "inns". He was graciously provided with food and shelter. Grateful for the innkeeper's hospitality he was unaware of the threat the evildoers posed to his safety.

After the evening meal he was shown to the room where he was to spend the night. Of course he looked forward with anticipation for a good night's rest.

As usual he knelt down to recite his evening prayers – a religious ritual firmly established in his deeply spiritual Christian upbringing. But as he knelt down he dropped his missile under the bed. As he raised the bed covers he froze with horror at the blood curdling sight before him. There, lying murdered, was his brother!!! Paralyzed with fear he escaped noiselessly through the window and fled or flew away from that accursed "inn".

How long this diabolic innkeeper had operated this evil practice, the story does not tell. Perhaps the ill-fated youth was the only traveler who survived to witness and report the heinous activities conducted in that infernal establishment.

The Whistler

Not all of these tales were based on reality. But nonetheless they were narrated as gospel truth. That was evidently the reason why those horror mysteries instilled such terror in the listener, and the hilarious comedies such sidesplitting laughter.

One of these mysterious fantasies concerned the students and teacher in a small rural school. The teacher was in the habit of punishing any transgression by putting the culprit in the cellar. A most frightening experience for the child! The isolation and darkness in those unfinished earth cellars must have been traumatic beyond endurance. At any rate, one child was in the habit of whistling incessantly from morning till night. No amount of persuasion or threat deterred him. His whistling was intolerable in the classroom. And so it was that the teacher cast him into the terrifying dungeon. However, before the teacher opened the trap door, he cried out most emphatically "Do not put me in there! I said, do not put me in there!" Thinking it was only a normal reaction, the teacher shoved him in and closed the trap door. At dismissal time, when all the other students had left, she opened the trap door and called out "You may come out now." There was no answer, yet from somewhere she could hear him whistling. Thinking that he had not heard her the first time, she called out again, louder "You may come out now. It is time to go home." Still no answer and still that weird, uncanny whistling sound!!! Tremors of fear enveloped her. Was he ill? She went down the ladder into the cellar and searched frantically everywhere. She looked for any opening by which he may have escaped. There was none! No windows! The dirt walls were intact! Panic seized her. Terrified, she dashed to the boy's home! And there, calm and composed, was the escapee. "How did you get out?" she demanded. "That is my secret," answered the boy. "But never, never, make me go in that dungeon again!"

Things returned to normal. Perhaps our hero was making a tremendous effort to restrain himself but soon he was whistling in the classroom again! And with the same results, the boy's warning, the escape and his presence when found at his home. Events have a tendency to repeat themselves. For the longest time, peace reigned at the school. Our hero was on his best behavior. But unfortunately he broke the rules again. "To the cellar," ordered the teacher, holding the trap door open. "I told you not to make me go down there ever again," he protested. His protestations were of no avail and down he went. However to the horror of both children and teacher his whistling could be heard rising from the cellar. Again, when he was called at dismissal time, he was nowhere to be found. Again the teacher rushed to his parents' home, but this time he was not there! The parents looked everywhere for him and so did his teacher and classmates. At last a search party was organized. They combed the whole district, but there was no sign of the boy! Not a trace! He had completely disappeared. Vanished without a trace. The legend claims that subsequent to the boy's disappearance the schoolhouse began to sink slowly into the ground until it was entirely submerged and disappeared. The most mystifying supernatural mystery was that the sound of the boy's eerie whistling never ceased. It was heard unremittingly in and around the schoolhouse while it was sinking and persisted even after it disappeared. The residents of the community claimed that the boy's disappearance was somewhat connected with the sinking of the schoolhouse. They were filled with apprehension and dread.

A Mysterious Apparition

The access to the family home led over a series of hills with varying degrees of elevation. The first rose to considerable heights. It was a sandy incline covered with brilliant multicolored stones. The hilltop to the right side of the road was heavily treed. The hawks had laid claim to this haven as their nesting territory. The next rise consisted of two low undulating hillocks facing each other. A little further up the road was a small mound covered with thick, rich, yellow sand. It was on this ridge that the blooming crocuses announced the first sign of spring. The last ridge was a steep slope covered with black clay that turned to mud in rainy weather. The steep slope upward combined with the mud made it almost impassable to scale. Many vehicles were stuck, buried hub deep and had to be pulled out of the mud and up the hill. Between the sandy mound and the clay incline there was a deep ravine.

Late one bitterly cold winter evening my dad was waiting anxiously for my mother's homecoming. Her tardiness, complemented by the fact that the temperature had plummeted way below zero, was perturbing. The elevation of the house allowed him to observe far down the road. Every now and then he interrupted his pacing to peer nervously through the window, which was thickly coated with hoarfrost.

As he gazed intently through the blurred glass he was aware of a light. It appeared to be far down the road, but was approaching steadily towards the house. Dad watched it as it came closer and closer, swaying to and fro to the rhythm of someone's footsteps. "Someone is coming over with a lantern," he thought. "Yet that light is much too bright to be from a lantern," he wondered. My dad stared at the gleaming light as it slowly kept coming, coming... At last it reached the top of the sandy mound. There it stopped. But only for an instant. In a flash it shot straight up into the sky and disappeared. My dad stood transfixed, spellbound, and unable to comprehend this amazing spectacle. He wondered if perhaps his agitation and anxiety had distorted his reasoning. Perhaps, he reasoned, the whole perception had been a figment of his imagination. So he decided to make an effort to establish whether or not his vision had been an illusion. He chose an evening when the temperature was extremely severe, way below zero, to begin his watch. At approximately the same time as before he began to see what appeared to be a man coming down the road carrying a lantern, as the light swayed regularly. The picture was so real that he thought his eyes must have deceived him previously. Strangely, however, the intense brilliance of the gleam blinded him. In spite of this he persisted. As before, the weird light kept coming up the road and again to my dad's amazement paused on the hilltop, shot straight up into the sky and vanished. Time after time this experiment was repeated, with the same results. Consequently the mysterious, inexplicable phenomenon was revealed to the rest of the family.

Humans are by nature skeptical. Although the father's word was gospel truth, each member doubted secretly whether such a thing was possible. Like doubting Thomas, each hoped to witness the strange spectacle personally in order to be convinced of its reality. Skepticism and curiosity compelled every member of the household to investigate this bizarre enigma. With varying degrees of angst each set out to do so. As a result, when the temperature was extremely severe, the window overlooking the ravine became the focal lookout point. Subsequently, most claimed to have viewed the extraordinary sight. One sister witnessed its apparition twice. The first time it followed its usual path, disappearing when it reached the sandy hillock. The immensity and radiance of the second apparition illuminated (or lit up) half the sky. It was astonishing! Many months later I had the pleasure of satisfying my curiosity and my skepticism. The sight filled me with amazement. Still it appeared to be too freakish, too bizarre to be true! And that cynicism remains even after witnessing this incredulous apparition personally. Doubting Thomas? Worst!

A Mysterious Healing

There is (believe it or not) another astonishing incidence that transpired in the neighbourhood. It was so incredible, so extraordinary that it was utterly incredible. Yet it was corroborated by all the folks who lived in the vicinity.

While the mother was occupied elsewhere doing household chores, a curious two year old girl (Marie) opened the cupboard where the cleaning material was kept. Then she opened and drank from a container filled with liquid lye.

Her piercing screams and shrieks alerted the panic stricken mother. Instantaneously the frantic mother rushed her to the doctor. Miraculously the child survived. There was however considerable damage to the walls of her whole digestive system. The doctor examined the child carefully. "Due to the severe damage to the digestive system it is imperative that the child be kept on a strict milk diet," he cautioned. "Any solid food would be fatal."

For many long years the child lived on a strict milk diet. The mother did not dare disobey the doctor's warning. Apparently the child was content and developed normally until she was about seven. During all these years she was never allowed to touch or partake of any solid food.

Meanwhile, during all those years, the mother prayed incessantly. At church, while doing her housework, during evening prayers, she never desisted!!! "Please God," she entreated, "my heart is filled with anguish because I feel responsible for my daughter's plight. I beseech you, grant an innocent child the healing from this horrid affliction." Throughout these extremely difficult times, the mother's faith remained unshaken as she prayed for the miraculous healing of her daughter.

One day, as she was, as usual, doing the endless tasks housekeeping demands, the mother heard her daughter calling her. "Mom," she said, "I am hungry. I want a piece of bread and butter." "Oh my darling child," retorted the alarmed mother. "You know that it is impossible for you to have bread and butter. You know what the doctor said! Bread and butter could make you very ill." "I want a piece of bread and butter," insisted the child. "I am hungry and that's what I will have." Subsequently, and to the mother's great horror, she buttered a piece of freshly baked bread with homemade butter and ate it. There were no repercussions! Henceforth and from that day onward, the child ate solid, normal food seated at the table with the rest of the family and never suffered any ill consequences. Folks claim that it was a miracle, an answer to the mother's faith in the benevolence of the Almighty.

Other remarkable incidences that occurred throughout her life made Marie a celebrity.

It is bizarre, uncanny, how some people's lives tend to be normal, uneventful and peaceful. Perhaps a little humdrum or boring. These fortunate souls can plan and delight in the magnanimous gifts that have been so bounteously showered upon them. There are others, unfortunately, whose lives are a series of earthshaking, momentous episodes, ensuing one on the heels of the other. And so it was with the heroine of this story. She was destined to have a rocky, eventful life. Marie grew to be a ravishing beauty. She was the envy of her female friends as she was extremely popular. Every gallant, chivalrous youth could only dream of becoming her "beau".

Unfortunately she fell madly in love with the priest's nephew, the deacon, of the parish. That old priest was a regular terror; so authoritarian was he to the stringent adherence of every church tradition and dictate. It may have been that both the couples' parents' and the inexorable old priest objected to the relationship, or perhaps that the young man was not interested. She pursued him, wooed him, but he repeatedly repulsed her courtesy and attentiveness toward him. For seemingly endless, miserable years she wept and mourned for her frigid lover, until she thought her heart would break! It was completely mystifying to all who knew her that such a beautiful, popular girl could have set her heart on one as insensitive and passionless. Yet it is characteristic of all earthly creatures, isn't it? Humans, especially, yearn for the unattainable, the pot of gold at the end of the rainbow! It must be true that persistence has its own reward. At long last the couple was wed. Whether the marriage was a success is unknown. No one will ever know because at the time divorce was unthinkable. The hell of an unhappy relationship had to be endured mercilessly!

The Unexplained

According to the local residents, the providential healing of Marie was not the only miracle that occurred in the environs. Folks in the surrounding area insist that they have witnessed innumerable phenomenon that are scientifically inexplicable. They maintain that these occurrences were a direct beneficent manifestation of divine mercy.

One of these miraculous incidences transpired in a small nearby village. As is often the case, the buildings in a small town are built very close together. There is little space between them. There were several stores, hotels, and other places of business situated in a rather congested area. The largest department store was located in a prominent central position of the town.

On one occasion, unfortunately, it happened that the whole building was engulfed in flames. The source of the fire was unknown and when it was discovered it was too late to salvage neither stock nor structure. Immediately behind the store and not more than two feet from it was a huge warehouse. Only a miracle could save it.

A fire, wherever or whenever it erupts, attracts the whole populace: men, women and children. That incidence was no exception!! Simultaneous to the flames, the crowd was engulfed by the electrifying, feverish agitation and consumed by its emotional perturbation. "Get the priest!" someone screamed, "Now!!" There was no need! The priest, alerted by the intense heat and the sight of blaze, had already rushed to the scene. To the amazement of all present he calmly walked and stood between the two buildings. Although the huge store was burned to the ground the warehouse remained, untouched! What prayer this courageous priest invoked and implored the Almighty must indeed have been formidable. Or did he simply say "I am the shield granted by divine power through which no fire will traverse."

Many years later that ill-fated merchant's life ended in tragedy. On his way to British Columbia, where he hoped to spend his holidays, he lost control of the car he was driving. The car plunged headlong down a treacherous mountain cliff. He, his daughter and her friend died as a result of the accident. The whole community, especially his customers, mourned the loss of a prominent citizen. Many speculated that the merchant had lost control because of exhaustion. Others believed that he had had a heart attack and had died before the accident.

The Unfathomable

Even in an immediate secluded entourage, there are mysteries that are beyond the realm of human understanding. Stranger than fiction is undeniably a side of my dad that was so private and inconspicuous that no one was aware of its mystifying implications.

What was most beguiling about this unassuming, unpretentious man was that he possessed a mysterious life saving gift. It was kept deeply concealed, unsuspected by anyone and never manifested, except in a desperate life threatening situation.

Looking back, my first awareness of this mystical phenomenon happened when I was very, very young. My brother George was chopping wood near the house when he accidentally inflicted a severe laceration on his foot. The wound was bleeding profusely, alarmingly! Every knowledgeable means was attempted to stop the bleeding without success! At last my dad was called. Whereupon he (my dad) proceeded, with a powerful blow, to drive the axe into the stump – the one that George had been using to chop the wood. The bleeding stopped instantly, the very moment when the axe was driven into the stump.

It was an awe-inspiring moment! Although everyone was amazed at this unusual, mysterious, astonishing performance, no one made any comments. Even more astonishing was the unspoken hush hush atmosphere, a feeling that this event should be kept under wrap and treated as insignificantly and inconspicuously as possible.

There was another occasion when this gift was manifested. Miles from any medical facility the pioneers were pretty well on their own when someone became ill. Fortunately most communities were endowed with someone who had extraordinary skills in the care of the sick. Armed and fortified with her medicine bag, filled with natural herbs, and her exceptional expertise, my grandmother, Emeralda, performed the role of the local doctor "the medicine woman!" In our district, a man, Good Sam, out of his generosity and compassion, had assumed the role of the local dentist. He was voluntarily saddled with, or more specifically, afflicted with, the task of extracting any offending teeth from an individual with a toothache.

On this particular occasion, a neighborhood girl had a tooth extracted. The extraction caused a great loss of blood, and regrettably even after she got home the bleeding could not be controlled. In desperation the mother sent one of the boys to our house wondering if my dad could help. Apparently all my father said was "Go home now, your sister is alright. She is not bleeding anymore." Low and behold, when the boy got home, the bleeding had stopped. The family claimed that it had stopped approximately at the time that my father had spoken these prodigious words.

An elderly lady in the district claimed that she could stop the burning agony of fire. She recounted an event in which a young girl had barely escaped with her life from a smoldering building. The girl had third and fourth degree burns all over her body. The pain was excruciating. She was summoned by someone who knew of her gift and was able to stop the anguish the victim was suffering instantly.

It is strange that individuals who possess such gifts refuse to discuss it. They claim that it is confidential and that they are not at liberty to disclose the manner in which they perform these miraculous deeds. They also claim that it is only upon the most exceptional and appropriate circumstances that they can share and confer the gift upon a particularly meritorious individual.

TALL TALES

At Sixes and Sevens

Some of these yarns (they must be yarns, surely!) are rooted, portray, and reek of the provincialism from which they emerge. Many are hilarious! A good storyteller will doubtlessly make his audience shriek with laughter, torn in stitches with these ridiculous tales. They are so nonsensical that to have the gall to repeat them, one must have the security of being barricaded behind the written word. At any rate, should the fortress crumble, I will throw caution to the winds and have the audacity to relate a few, at my own risk.

In Quebec, during the early part of the 19th century, most people spoke French exclusively. That is still the case in many parts of the province, as the students were not given the opportunity to learn English. It was not part of the curriculum. In the rural areas, this was not a problem, as everyone spoke the same language. The only contact these people had with the English speaking world was with traveling door-to-door salesmen. Most of these salesmen spoke English only and were unable to communicate with the local homeowners. However, one salesman happened to be French. Confident, he knocked at the door of the first house. When he was admitted the conversation that ensued went as follows: Salesman: Bonjour, madame! (Good afternoon, madam). Lady: M.je ne parle pas l'Anglais! (Sir, I do not speak English). Salesman: Mais, madame, je vous parle Francais! (But, madam, I am speaking French to you). Lady: M je ne parle pas l'Anglais! (Sir, I do not speak English). Salesman: Mais, madame, je vous dis que je vous parle Francois! (But, madam, I am telling you that I am speaking French to you).

This conversation went on and on. The exasperated salesman tried in vain to emphasize "I am telling you that I am speaking French", to no avail. The poor woman was so fixated that she was unable to hear him (maybe she had had one of these mornings when everything goes wrong!) At last the unfortunate salesman shrugged his shoulders, shook his head, and went on his way, unable to comprehend the absurdity of the encounter. No one would condemn this gentleman if he talked to himself shaking his head in a daze all the way to the next house. No one could blame him either wondering if he had lost his mind.

The next unbelievable story was even more weird and it kept getting worse, if such a thing could be earthly possible. It is no wonder because it is their absurdity that makes the tales so hilarious!

In a small village located in the midst of a farming community lived a young, robust lad whose rapacious appetite was insatiable. He (so the story goes) devoured everything in sight, yet never succeeded in satisfying the fierce craving constantly gnawing at his entrails.

Well, one fine day, just before dawn, being ravenous, he proceeded to make his early morning breakfast rounds. As was customary, he stopped at the first house, and as the family was in the process of having breakfast, he was invited to join in. He gratefully accepted. He ate as much as he dared within the bounds of propriety and left.

Then he stopped at a second house. Was it a coincidence that they (the residents) also were having breakfast? Graciously he sat and accompanied this family at their first meal of the day and left. This ritual continued throughout the early hours of the day. When he had consumed the fifth, or perhaps the seventh meal, he stopped at a house where the lady was in the process of making pancakes for her husband and children. Pancakes was (and is) of course one of the Quebecois' favorite delicacy. And besides, no one was ever-turned away hungry from a French Canadian home at the time. So our hero joined in the regale (from the threads handed down in the tale it was his first visit in that particular home). The kind hostess had made enough pancakes to feed her family, so she proceeded to make some for her guest. One, two, three…twenty, twenty-one…on and on…. After each batch she would stare incredulously at her guest and wonder, "Will he ever be satisfied? How can he eat that much?" Finally, exhausted, after the twenty-seventh pancake she exclaimed, exasperated "Do you know, sir, that you have eaten twenty-seven pancakes?" Subsequently the young man rose, thanked his host, and left, indignant! "Well!" he commented, outraged, to the next neighbor, hopefully the last one on his early morning breakfast rounds, "I was <u>so</u> insulted, I left without breakfast!!!"

In the community where my parents lived there was not only a gourmand, a shrew, an outstanding runner, a lady with a one-track mind, but it was also blessed with the proverbial town thief.

Everyone in the neighborhood knew that this man was the culprit who was robbing them blind. Yet no one had been able to catch him red handed. For this man was not an ordinary robber. He had the finesse, the charm and the cunning of the fox. So the people accepted his shenanigans as an inexorable matter of course.

This shrewd brigand had all the elegance, the flamboyance of the ancient gentleman pirate. For he robbed his neighbors with such a flare, such a ceremonial approach that the incidence was worthy of any flourishing theatrical performance.

His uncle was becoming increasingly alarmed at the dwindling number of sheep in his flock. He was convinced that he knew who was culpable of stealing his sheep. So he decided to verify his suspicions.

One evening he hid in the barn where the sheep were kept and waited. Sure enough, at approximately midnight, his nephew entered the barn. Instead of taking a sheep and leaving furtively as any normal self respecting thief would do, this malfeasant sat down and started talking to the sheep; addressing his speech to the ram in particular. Still the uncle remained silent and watched and listened in amazement. The nephew:

Well, Mr. Ram, have you a prize healthy ewe for sale this evening? The ram (impersonated by the nephew) I have several. Nephew: I want nothing but the very best. Ram: The one in the corner of the barn. She is the best in the flock. Nephew: She is indeed most beautiful. How much do you want for her? Ram: Fifty. Nephew: That's outrageous! I'll not pay a cent more than twenty-five. Ram: That ewe is worth twice that much. But I'll let you have her for forty-five. Nephew: That's too much.

And so the negotiations went on and on till the early hours of the morning until both agreed on the fair price of thirty dollars. Whereupon the thief laid down some makeshift money, loaded the ewe on his shoulders and departed. The uncle still did not disclose his presence.

The following evening our crafty robber invited the whole neighbourhood to participate in an elaborate feast. The host seated his uncle at the most prestigious seat at the table and treated him as the honored and special guest.

"Help yourself, uncle," he kept entreating over and over. "Don't be shy. It's all yours." "Well, of course it's mine. It's my sheep," thought the vexed uncle. "I am the founder of this feast."

The legend never did mention whether or not this bad actor was ever apprehended. Perhaps it was felt that his dramatic performances compensated for his crimes.

Beelzebub (At It Again!)

In the early part of the 19th century and previous to that era, some traditionalists (my father included) were dead set against "la danse" (dancing). They claimed that it was the invention of, and an activity performed by Lucifer, surrounded by his entourage.

A legend has it that two sisters longed to go dancing with their friends. The excitement, the joviality, made them wish to join in the merriment. But no matter how they pleaded and begged, their parents were indomitable in their refusal to let them go. It happened one day that a friend persuaded the girls to accompany him in spite of the parents' aversion and ruling against it. When the evening of the ball finally arrived, the friend, handsomely dressed in black, and truly a most charming and elegant escort, appeared at the door. He was driving four jet-black horses pulling a magnificent coach. Dressed in their most delicate finery, the two sisters were ecstatic with joy. Swift as the wind they were driven to the ballroom, where they proceeded at once to join in the merriment. The revelry was at its height, the music loud and lilting, and the guests dancing wildly (with glee) to the regular beat of the music.

The handsome escort had chosen his partner, one of the sisters, and was spinning her around. She realized, suddenly, that he was still wearing his gloves and to her horror long, sharp, terrifying claws were protruding through them. Petrified she tried to disengage herself from his grasp. All her efforts were in vain. He dragged her out of the building to where the coach and the horses were tied. The guests froze in terror, too stunned to realize what was actually happening. Soon, however, everyone rushed outside, hoping to rescue the ill-fated girl. To their amazement there was no sign of the girl, the escort, horses or coach. And in the spot where the horses had stood pawing impatiently at the ground, was but a gush, a torrent of flames that was submerged and disappeared as they stood gazing, terrified, in amazement! Needless to say, dancing was not a popular activity for many years subsequent to this catastrophic event.

Upon closer examination of these frightening legends, it is quite evident that they were didactic in nature. Because of their horrifying content, they were most effective when used to coerce conformity to the norm by means of terror.

CONCLUSION

While ruminating upon the path the voyage of my life has led me, I realized that it was long, long years later that I finally returned to the home site of my childhood. A scene that was so poignantly filled with memories and that was now a scene of desolation. As I gazed upon the ravages that time and man had wrought upon every figment of my dreams, a feeling of anguish and sadness overwhelmed me.

Yet, although the concrete evidence of the log house and all its entourage had been obliterated, it remained crystal clear, there, before my mind's eyes. And the people long ago departed, who walked upon these precious soils, though not present in substance, their essence nonetheless were still subsiding and abiding within me, incessantly, persistently treading upon my heels wherever I go.

After years of toil and struggle, the homestead, e.g. the farm, was abandoned. Funds for the repayment of the mortgage and the yearly taxes were unavailable. The new owner effaced, wiped off the face of the earth by burning to the ground every trace of human habitation. By this time, most of the family, except Raymond and Cecile, had long left and sought their separate ways elsewhere. They relocated and settled in the small North Saskatchewan town of Leoville, where both Jean and Juliette resided. They bought a small lot and installed a small house upon it. This humble residence became their temporary home. The only apparent and recognizable possessions brought from the farm were the organ, the spinning wheel, the clock, Dad's rocking chair, and the cows!!! The cows, that at milking time, Raymond cursed so vehemently!!

When all the family possessions had been arranged in their proper places, and the family's rituals had been established, the sense of entity reigned once more in the household. Both for the residents and the wandering members! There was Mother at the spinning wheel, and there were her books, magazines, and newspapers, strewn all over the house. And there was Dad, leisurely smoking his pipe, seated in his favorite rocking chair. And there was Mother's indefatigable passion of unselfish hospitality. But as Juliette commented significantly, there was something lacking, something that had been ever present in days of yore. The melodies that once emanated from a joyful heart and had once held this home in harmony had vanished. Perhaps those songs had been wrenched from her heart by the sense of futility and hopelessness.

Hélène's wedding was celebrated in that home. Every effort had been made, in spite of the humble environment, to create the desired decorum and propriety suitable for such a momentous ceremony. (Hélène was a most respected and esteemed member of the family.) It was ostensibly a huge success. (I was unable to attend).

For some obscure reasons, my parents decided to leave Leoville. It was most likely for economic reasons. Excepting for the revenue from the dairy products, there was no other available source of income. These cows had always been a point of contention. It was also most difficult to obtain the necessary pasture for them. It was probably a great relief to dispose of them.

So they decided to move to Toxedo Island, west of British Columbia. My Dad and Raymond were to gather huckleberry branches as a source of income. Florists created an extensive demand for this product. It was used to embellish their floral arrangements and designs. Furthermore the labor involved was not overly cumbersome. They built themselves a shelter on the island and for some time they seemed to live in peace.

It was while they lived on Toxedo Island that my mother passed away. From my earliest recollections she had suffered numerous afflictions and had never enjoyed good health. Never complaining, unselfishly considering the needs of everyone else before hers, besides refusing medical attention when seriously ill, contributed to her demise. She must have had a premonition or sense that death was at the door. She was incessantly repeating, "All I ask is that I remain on earth until all my children have been provided for, and do not need me any more." That is precisely what transpired. Although Raymond was still living at home when she passed away, he was a man and could fend for himself.

Through the years she had kept painfully performing whatever household duties her frail physique enabled her to do. Besides she was constantly pondering over means and ways that would engender her family's survival. Business meetings, community functions, grocery shopping trips, all augmented her innumerable schedule. Furthermore she was compelled to travel to and from these functions in a horse drawn vehicle, an open sleigh in winter and a wagon in summer. How insufferable these trips must have been! There were compensations. Peering anxiously through the windows, were many eyes, joyously anticipating her return, for there always was a treat.

During her last pregnancy she suffered from toxemia. As was customary she refused to think of herself and to seek medical advice and care. The symptoms got progressively worse. After her confinement she was hospitalized for a considerable length of time. The child did not survive. His physical condition was so severe that the doctors in attendance had no hope for him. The child was sent home. This ill-advised decision created tremendous trauma and anguish in the household. Young and inexperienced, those who were to care for the infant had never been completely responsible for the care of a healthy baby, let alone care for an infant who was fatally ill.

Delirious most of the time while in the hospital, upon her return home, my mother joked about the illusions she had experienced. Once she imagined that a formidable enemy was about to invade the premises. She also visualized an immense hole in the floor of her ward. Yet the nuns seemed insensible and unperturbed by the urgency of the situation. "Yes, yes, we'll attend to the matter immediately," they'd patiently reply to her intense and persistent entreaties.

The toxemia damaged her kidneys to such an extent that their function was seriously impaired. The poisoned blood flowing through her body was most injurious and detrimental to the heart. Consequently she suffered from an acute heart disease. The doctors prescribed a drug called digitalis to control the ill effects of the disease. The least effort rendered her incapacitated and subject to fainting spells. Even washing dishes proved to be too strenuous. Yet she never, not even once, complained! However she deeply resented the fact that her weak kidneys prohibited the use of coffee, tea, and especially salt.

While on the island she decided to go to Vancouver in order to try a well advertised treatment by a reputable chiropractor. Returning to the hotel room after one of these treatments, she called Cécile, who was at the time working in that establishment. She implored her to summon the family; she felt her time was near. When Cécile returned to the room, she was gone. The trauma, the anguish that Cécile experienced was so severe that she failed to notify any of the family except (mercifully) my dad and Raymond. This was most painful to all.

Her demise left a void so deep, so painful, that time has failed to heal the distress of the wound.

Yet, we should not weep, for the essence of who she was will live forever. Like the mustard seed, the gifts that she has sown are scattered and thrive in the hearts of those she has left to continue her pilgrimage. Her wisdom is channeled and spread through the voice of some chosen one. It is a voice that transmits and reveals its brilliance and through which she continues to be a ray of light illuminating the gloom.

Her benevolence is glaringly (sometimes damningly) conspicuous in one who stands stark naked having given his <u>all</u> to appease the desperation manifested in the eyes of those who hunger.

Her essence is manifested in every child born clutching fiercely a book in his grasp.

She exists in the soul of each who loves music, song, and the arts. Alas, all that is fine and beautiful.

Her presence is in all those who stand firm for justice and strive to crush the shackles of bondage, ever proclaiming freedom!

It may be that John McCrae chose my mother to carry the "torch" he so brilliantly illustrated in his poem "In Flanders Field". But her weapons were not the weapons of war, but a piece of bread and a glass of water. "These are," she thought, "more lethal than the sword in the destruction of hatred and war. They are exceedingly more powerful in creating the bonds of brotherhood and peace."

And so, throughout her life, she cast her bread upon the waters, her life upon the waves, threw caution to the winds, trusting that the wind and tide would turn, bringing back all the yearnings and wonders all humans aspire. She was a light forever guiding the path that leads out of the darkness.

She had indeed thrown caution to the winds; cast her bread upon the shimmering waters. And upon the scintillating waves, every crystal drop still glittering with the brilliance of the wisdom it still bears.

EPILOGUE

After my mother's death, my dad returned to Saskatchewan. For some time he lived in the Leoville home with Marie-Anne, caring for her children. When Marie-Anne left, he went back to British Columbia.

Subsequently my dad lived in his own little cabin provided by and near my sister Hélène's home in Maple Ridge, B.C. He must obviously have relished the peace, the quiet that he had long awaited during all these tumultuous years. Nonetheless he must have missed my mother intensely. At times, while he watched television, listening to his favorite singer, he would comment, "He or she is wonderful, but no one can even hope to compare with your mother's beautiful singing voice." Many times he declared to anyone who happened to be visiting at the moment, "You never know how to treasure and appreciate what you possess until you lose it. And when you lose it the pain is devastating."

He enjoyed company. During these visits he never failed to entertain his guests with his fantastic, hilarious tales. For he never did lose his gift as a storyteller. Many times his listeners' whole bodies (frames?) were contorted with laughter. During his eighty-nine years he remained in good health! He was confined in the hospital for only a week during his very last days. Almost till the very end he cared for himself and for his little cabin. It can be truly said that "he died with his boots on".

Along the tumultuous path, the voyage of life has left me some souvenirs filled with euphoria while others with a deep sense of sadness and loss. Yet there are those that instill a sense of accomplishment and are profoundly rewarding. For instance, the role many of my relatives have performed in the history of Western Canada.

My parents would be overjoyed to realize that the members of their family have shed the repressing shackles of deprivation, that they have stripped themselves bare and cast aside its harrowing portent. The log shack is a thing of the past – along with the washboard, the plunger, and scrub brush, even the clothespins. These have become antiques. They are regarded as items of great value. This is best illustrated in the words of a ten year old boy – "I wish I had lived when you were young, Grandma! I could have scrubbed my clothes on a washboard. It would have been so much fun!!!"

Little did that child know what transpired. Little did he comprehend the ramifications that came along with that "fun".

My parents would be most gratified to see that their children and grandchildren live in comfortable homes equipped with every facet of modern technology. The modern generation will accept nothing but excellence. That is especially true of the young. In recent years the trend has been to prioritize the external and material aspect of human aspirations. In the frantic rage to provide nothing but the best for their children, some parents chose what they thought would facilitate their mode or style of living and bring them happiness. Many chose to provide for their external needs rather than their ecstatic spiritual needs. This is indeed most regrettable. No matter how splendid the mansion with ornaments gilded in gold, unless the mind is receptive and appreciative of beauty and splendor, the manor will be viewed as barren, empty – as is the mind that wanders aimlessly within its confines. The transience and superficiality of gold and silver is like sand slithering through the fingers. For the spiritual needs are the most critical in a human being's unquenchable quest for peace and happiness. Philosophers, meta-physicians are those who envisioned the depth and crucial significance of this truth. My Grandfather Savard and my parents, in their wisdom, understood and lived by its dictates. Grandfather knew and understood when, on a meager income, and with tremendous sacrifices, sent his children to the most elite schools. My mother, throughout her existence and in spite of the lack of material possessions, taught and enlightened the spiritual aspect of existence. A woman, who while spinning yarn for survival, taught poetry. A woman who taught music, singing, drama and especially the love of the written word. One whose home was bursting with books and musical instruments! Such a person knew, understood, and fully appreciated the significance of spirituality. For spirituality encompasses more and has greater depths than religious faith - the belief in God and everlasting life. It encompasses all that separates and distinguishes humanity from all other animal species. It encompasses the consciousness of the ecstatic aspect of existence – the ability to rise above the physical and appreciate to the full the needs of the spirit. Love of one's brother and of beauty, music, literature, art, and drama. It is with this perceptive spiritual wisdom that one floats upon the wings of enlightenment and is able to be transported beyond and above the concrete and the real. These precious spiritual gifts are embedded within the very depths of the soul. They're securely guarded, impervious to time and human chicanery. They're to be coveted – a solace even unto the grave.

Some authorities claim that artistic expression must be cushioned by financial stability. According to this theory, our community was exceptional, perhaps even unconventional, for it did not in the least fit this mold. Most were of mediocre means. Few were financially secure, yet musical talent abounded irrespective of economics. In fact, music poured forth from the hearts of the poorest. It may be that the whole community was obsessed, not in the accumulation of material wealth and prestige, but on the accumulation of the treasures manifested and emanating from the arts. Perhaps forsaking gold and silver they rejoiced in the rapture, the ecstasy of life itself expressed in song and melody. It was the voice in which they could express the longings and wonders inherent in their hearts.

In times of dire struggles for mere survival these internal assets provided the pioneers with the strength to carry on and the comfort to assuage the rigors of a hostile environs. This intense passion, this voracious appetite for intellectual pleasure was solely and evidently what enabled my grandfather, and especially my mother, to survive. May they joyfully contemplate from their celestial upstairs domain their loved ones; for they possess both a mansion to shelter their bodies and a spiritual mansion for the "bien etre" of the mind. The pioneers have prepared the soil and made it possible for their loved ones to luxuriate in the possession of both mansions. To them we should be eternally grateful.

It is with great pride that I contemplate the contributions that the members of my family performed towards the opening and building of the Canadian West. My mother was, of course, the prime mover. For she was the one who instigated the resettlement in the west. She pleaded, begged, and coaxed until the decision was final. Then my parents packed their bags and relocated. It was not without serious repercussions however. For my father was never convinced that the move would be or was to their advantage. Afterward he bitterly regretted the fact that he had been persuaded to proceed with such a rash venture. Consequently my mother had to endure his constant recriminations.

Besides being almost totally responsible for the relocation, my mother brought with her the talents and artistic skills she had been taught by the dedicated sisters at the convent. These skills brought pleasure and greatly enriched the lives of all those in her entourage.

In spite of his reluctance and misgivings, it was perhaps my dad's contributions that proved to be the most extensive. Like all other pioneers he cleared and prepared the land for cultivation on his homestead. But what was more significant and permanent was his "input" into the building of the railroad across Canada. Every winter my dad succeeded in fulfilling a contract for "railway ties". It formed the foundation or base upon which the transcontinental rails were laid and secured.

Traveling across Canada by train, it is undeniably exhilarating to contemplate the fact that the rails upon which this train is moving were laid and secured on some labor emanating from my father's hands.

It is also most gratifying to remember that on that memorable, historical event when the last spike was driven to secure the rail at the terminal, my grandfather Savard was among that valiant crew.

My brother John cleared and opened up vast areas of land and prepared it for cultivation. From dawn till dusk he sat on a "cat" (caterpillar) clearing the land, not only on his homestead but for many other pioneers in his community. He was also among those who freighted in the northern part of Saskatchewan. These freighters were instrumental in making the Canadian people realize the tremendous value of the resources inherent in the north. They also helped in the development of these resources.

The growth and development of the commercial centers such as Big River, Prince Albert and others depended on these courageous men. They braved the hazards of the untrodden wilderness, the excruciating temperatures, the fatigue, the loneliness, in order to develop the resources of the north.

At Ile a' la Cross, Hélène, using her skill as a nurse cared for the sick. Later, in Mackenzie, B.C., as a public health nurse, she cared for the native children's health. It was utterly deplorable that, unlike teachers, nurses did not have a union. Therefore they were not entitled to a pension when they retired. It is almost incredible that after caring for the sick forty-three years Hélène did not receive a pension. She was and always will be first and foremost a nurse, the embodiment of dedicated service to others. Her devotion, dedication and care is remarkable. Yet it remains unappreciated and unrewarded. It is hopefully anticipated that those she so diligently, devotedly cared for, the sick, treasure her memory in their hearts.

Many others dear to my memory contributed in their own particular way to the building of Canada, as it exists today. For instance, the way my grandparents spread the word of God. Not in word but in deed. Providing for everyone's needs except for their own, throughout their lives.

It would be gratifying were it feasible, to celebrate and perpetuate the life of every meritorious person and every single virtuous deed. Alas, it cannot be!

Throughout my life I have been deeply troubled and lived in torment concerning my parents' financial struggle. This tribulation has incessantly disturbed my rest and manifested itself in my dreams. For night after night in that same recurring dream I am frantically and desperately seeking far and wide for a suitable home for my parents. It is a never-ending search and continues throughout the night. One after another the dwellings prove unsuitable and are rejected. Castles as too extravagant, high rises as inaccessible, unfinished structures as impractical. Sometimes in a frenzy I try to remodel and clean some building scrubbing and painting all night long. At times just when one dwelling seems appropriate and suitable and think that I have succeeded at long last, I wake up, exhausted, unable to fulfill my goal. Other times I hear myself saying to them, "Do not worry. From now on I will provide you with all your needs." Strange! Weird! Yet the fact that this was beyond the bounds of all possibility when they were alive fills me with anguish. After all these years the fulfillment of that promise has finally become feasible. Alas, it is too late!

Perhaps there is a message in those dreams. A communiqué incognizant to my limited earthly intelligence, that something crucial was left undone, a stone was left unturned, and that the heavens are vainly trying to communicate to me. Or is it simply a desire to ascertain their home in my heart. Oh! That I could only decipher the depth of its significance!

BIBLIOGRAPHY

1. Casgrain Henri Raymond: "La Jangleuse" 1999
   Catholic Encyclopedia, Copyright Kevin Knight 1999
   Collection Dollard Beauchemin Library 1922

2. DeLamarre l'Abbe' Elzear: Victor DeLamarre
   Published at Quebec November 1998
   Bibliothegue National de Quebec

3. Dube' Wilfrid: Beaupre' Edward
   Published Montreal Quebec National Film Board 1987

4. Franklin Martin Cyr Louis
   Montreal Nord Quebec, Published by La Presse 1980
   Memoirs de l'homme le plus Fort du Monde

5. Sulte Benjamin: Histoire de Montferand
   University d Attawa: Joe Montferand
   Centre de recheiche civilization canadienne francaise

6. The Holy Bible: Luke 22 & 27

7. Shakespeare William: "Hamlet"

8. Shakespeare William: "The Tempest"

9. Most of the incidences related in this book are true life experiences

10. Others are French Canadian legends originating in Quebec or south
    of the border

11. The Development of Education in Canada by Charles E. Phillips
    1957 W. J. Gage & Company Ltd., Toronto, Copyright 1957

12. The Encyclopedia of Education, Lee C. Deighton V.2
    The MacMillan Co. & The Free Press
    1971 Copyright – Cromwell Collier Educational Corporation 1971

Edwards Brothers Malloy
Oxnard, CA USA
September 8, 2014